GLUTEN-FREE
SOURDOUGH

For Everyone

PRACTICAL GUIDE WITH FOOLPROOF TECHNIQUES FOR FLAVORFUL, SOFT & FLUFFY ARTISAN BREAD

INCLUDES SPECIAL SINGLE-FLOUR RECIPES IDEAL FOR BEGINNERS

DIANE ROMANO

EXCLUSIVE FREE BONUS FOR YOU!

Don't forget to DOWNLOAD IT

JUMP NOW TO THE END OF THE BOOK

and scan the QR CODE!

TABLE OF CONTENT

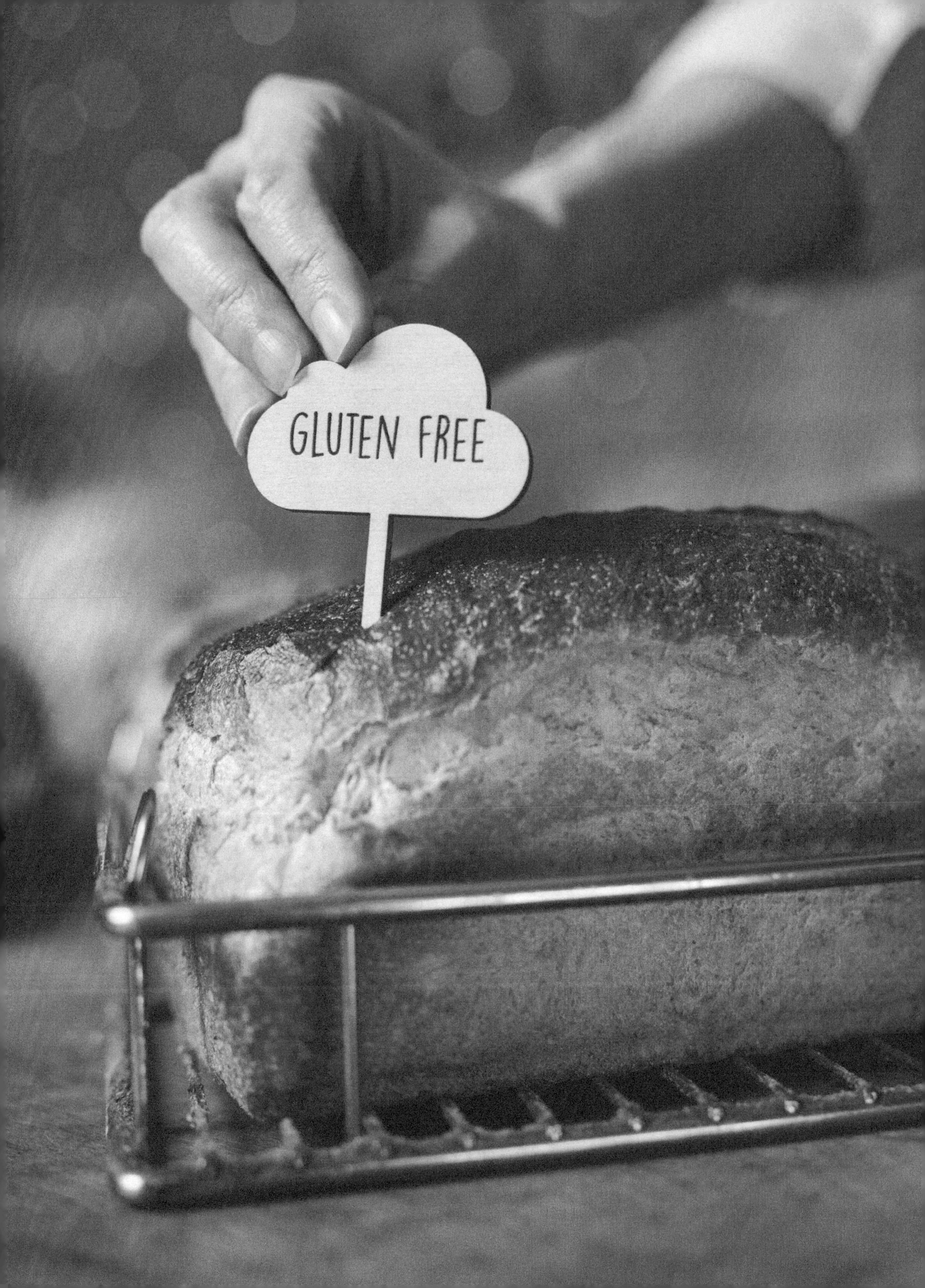
GLUTEN FREE

INTRODUCTION

Hello, I'm Diane Romano, an experienced cook with Italian roots, deeply influenced by the rich culinary traditions of my heritage. I have always baked bread following the Italian tradition with sourdough. For the past 30 years, since my daughter was diagnosed with celiac disease, I have completely transformed my cooking approach to adapt to a gluten-free diet.

This change challenged me to bring the qualities of traditional bread—its taste, texture, and aroma—into gluten-free baking, striving to recreate that authentic experience for my family.

It wasn't an easy path. I spent countless hours in the kitchen, experimenting with gluten-free flours and facing disappointment with gummy loaves and rock-hard rolls.

As many of you know, working with leavened products means dealing with numerous variables like temperature, humidity, and the types of flours used. However, not everyone realizes that when you decide to enter the fascinating world of sourdough, you're adding an even more critical variable: the natural leavening process.

The most important process in making good bread is handed over to a living organism. Its vitality, strength—or as I like to say, its "character"—vary from starter to starter, influenced by a multitude of factors.

So, Diane, are you saying that making good gluten-free sourdough bread is something only experts can do? Absolutely not!

That's precisely why I wrote this book: to compile all my decades of experience into a practical step-by-step guide that enables anyone to succeed in baking fragrant and delicious bread.

But there's something I want to tell you right from the start: no matter how well-tested my methods and recipes are, bread baking—especially with sourdough—isn't just about following a recipe meticulously; it's about intuition and adaptability.

Even for me, it wasn't easy. With patience and determination, I kept trying and failing until I finally achieved a soft bread with a crispy crust and the unmistakable aroma that reminded us of traditional bread.

Throughout this book, I'll provide as much information as possible to help you navigate these variables and achieve perfect loaves. However, it's important to remember that patience is key in this process. Patience is what can make the difference between a beautiful loaf and an inedible brick. So, arm yourself with patience, and let your instincts guide you: together, we'll explore the wonderful world of gluten-free bread, one step at a time.

THE SCIENCE OF SOURDOUGH

Before diving into the practical aspects, it's essential to first understand the theory behind sourdough starter. I know it may seem tedious, but believe me, understanding what's happening beneath the surface is crucial to mastering this remarkable method of baking. By knowing how sourdough works, you'll be better equipped to handle the variables that influence your bread, and you'll develop the intuition needed to adjust and adapt as you go.

Sourdough is a natural leavening agent composed of flour and water that hosts a symbiotic culture of wild yeasts and lactic acid bacteria. This mixture provides both the rise and distinctive flavor of the bread. Unlike commercial yeast, which relies on a single species, sourdough uses a diverse community of microorganisms found in the environment and on the grains.

Key Components of Sourdough Starter:

- **Flour:** The type of flour influences the starter's activity and flavor. Whole grain flours, like brown rice or millet, contain more nutrients and wild yeasts than refined flours, making them ideal for cultivating a robust starter. Flour provides sugars and starches that feed the yeasts and bacteria.

- **Water:** Water provides the medium for yeast and bacteria to activate and interact. The quality of the water can affect the starter; it's generally best to use non-chlorinated, filtered, or bottled water to avoid inhibiting microbial growth. The hydration level of the starter can also impact its consistency and activity, but these aspects are more about fine-tuning as the starter develops.

- **Wild Yeasts:** These are naturally occurring yeasts present in the flour and the environment. They differ from commercial yeast because they are more diverse and contribute to a broader range of flavors and fermentation characteristics. Wild yeasts are responsible for producing carbon dioxide, which creates the bubbles that make the dough rise.

- **Lactic Acid Bacteria:** Alongside the wild yeasts, lactic acid bacteria play a crucial role in sourdough starter. These bacteria produce lactic and acetic acids, which give sourdough its characteristic tangy flavor and help to preserve the bread by lowering its pH. This acidity also strengthens the dough's structure, making it more resilient and enhancing its texture.

YEAST AND BACTERIA SYNERGY

The fermentation process in sourdough involves a complex interplay between wild yeasts and lactic acid bacteria, which coexist in a symbiotic relationship. When flour and water are mixed, it creates an environment that activates yeasts and bacteria on the grains and in the air. As the starter matures, these microorganisms multiply, establishing a stable culture.

Wild yeasts in sourdough starter are responsible for leavening the bread. They feed on sugars in the flour, breaking them down through glycolysis, producing carbon dioxide and ethanol. The carbon dioxide forms bubbles in the dough, causing it to rise and create an airy structure. This gradual leavening develops complex flavors, unlike the rapid rise seen with commercial yeast.

Lactic acid bacteria also play a crucial role in fermentation by metabolizing sugars into lactic and acetic acids. They thrive in an acidic environment, which they help create by lowering the pH of the dough. This lower pH preserves the dough by inhibiting harmful bacteria and enhances yeast activity.

The acids produced by the lactic acid bacteria contribute significantly to the characteristics of sourdough bread. Lactic acid provides a mild tangy flavor, while acetic acid adds sharper notes. These acids also strengthen the dough by tightening the gluten network (or structural components in gluten-free breads), improving texture and quality.

The synergy between wild yeasts and lactic acid bacteria makes sourdough unique. This interaction causes the dough to rise, imparts depth of flavor, complex aroma, satisfying chew, and improves keeping qualities.

HOW SOURDOUGH STARTER IMPROVES GLUTEN-FREE BREAD

Baking gluten-free bread poses challenges, from achieving the right texture to developing flavor. Sourdough starter is a game-changer, helping overcome many hurdles of gluten-free baking.

Sourdough starter does more than leaven; it enhances various aspects of gluten-free bread, resulting in a superior product.

Let's take a closer look at the key ways in which sourdough starter contributes to improving gluten-free bread:

- **Improving Structure:** In traditional bread, gluten provides structure and elasticity. Gluten-free flours lack this, often resulting in denser loaves. Sourdough fermentation produces carbon dioxide and organic acids, which improve rise and crumb cohesion. The acids strengthen the dough matrix, enhancing stability and texture even without gluten.

- **Enhancing Flavor:** Sourdough starter enriches gluten-free bread with a complex flavor profile that is hard to achieve with commercial yeast. Wild yeasts and lactic acid bacteria produce organic compounds like acids, alcohols, and esters, adding depth and character. The wild yeasts and lactic acid bacteria in the starter produce a variety of organic compounds, including acids, alcohols, and esters, which add depth and character to the bread. This tangy, nuanced flavor significantly enhances gluten-free bread, which can otherwise be bland.

- **Improving Digestibility and Enhancing Nutrition:** During fermentation, the lactic acid bacteria work to partially break down complex carbohydrates and reduce antinutritional factors, such as phytic acid, present in many gluten-free flours. This process helps increase the bioavailability of essential minerals like iron, zinc, and magnesium, making the nutrients in the bread more accessible to the body.

  The acids produced during sourdough fermentation still lower the pH of the dough, which can deactivate certain enzyme inhibitors that might otherwise complicate digestion. This contributes to a gentler digestive experience, especially for those sensitive to various components of gluten-free grains.

  Fermentation also enhances nutrition by producing B vitamins and antioxidants, and lowers the glycemic index by reducing fermentable sugars, making it a healthier option for managing blood sugar. This thorough fermentation not only supports better digestion but also optimizes nutrient absorption, resulting in a more wholesome and nourishing loaf.

- **Extending Shelf Life:** Sourdough starter extends bread's shelf life. The acids produced during fermentation lower the pH, inhibiting mold growth and retaining moisture, which slows staling. As a result, sourdough bread stays fresher longer than bread made with commercial yeast, reducing the need for preservatives.

THE VARIABLES THAT INFLUENCE SOURDOUGH STARTER

Sourdough starter is a dynamic culture that evolves over time. A young starter, within the first few weeks, lacks a fully balanced ecosystem of yeasts and bacteria. During this stage, the microbial community is stabilizing, leading to inconsistent leavening and unpredictable flavors. Young starters often have a milder taste and may produce denser bread due to less gas production.

After several weeks of regular feedings, a starter matures and develops a stable balance of microorganisms. A mature starter has a well-established population of yeasts and bacteria, resulting in reliable fermentation, stronger leavening, and a pronounced flavor. This balance is crucial in gluten-free baking, contributing to better rise, texture, and the tanginess characteristic of sourdough.

FACTORS THAT CAN ALTER THE ACTIVITY AND VITALITY OF SOURDOUGH STARTER

- **Temperature:** Temperature plays a crucial role in the activity of your sourdough starter. The ideal temperature range is between 75°F and 82°F (24°C and 28°C), ensuring that yeasts and bacteria remain active.

  Below 70°F (21°C), fermentation can take significantly longer, and the starter may become sluggish, leading to underdeveloped dough and poor rise. This can result in denser bread with less lift.

  In contrast, temperatures above 82°F (28°C) accelerate yeast activity but can lead to over-acidification, affecting flavor and texture. Maintaining a stable, warm environment for your starter is crucial, as sudden temperature changes can cause inconsistent fermentation.

- **Type of Flour:** The type of flour used to feed the starter influences its activity. Gluten-free flours like rice, sorghum, or millet have unique nutrient profiles that affect starter behavior. Whole grain flours contain more nutrients and microorganisms, boosting activity and flavor, while refined flours may lack these nutrients, requiring additional care or supplementation.

  Avoid using commercial flour blends like measure-for-measure or 1-to-1 gluten-free flours, as they are highly refined and lack nutrients. They often contain additives like xanthan gum or preservatives, which hinder beneficial microbial growth. For a thriving starter, use single-ingredient, whole grain flours.

- **Feeding Frequency:** Regular feeding is essential for maintaining an active and healthy sourdough starter. The frequency of feedings depends on the ambient conditions and the specific needs of the starter. More frequent feedings provide a steady supply of fresh nutrients, promoting robust yeast and bacterial activity, while less frequent feedings can lead to an accumulation of acids and depletion of nutrients, weakening the starter.

- **Hydration Levels:** Hydration, or the water-to-flour ratio, impacts starter activity. Higher hydration encourages faster fermentation and more bacterial activity, leading to a tangier flavor. A stiffer starter ferments more slowly, resulting in a milder taste. Adjusting hydration in gluten-free starters is crucial, as different flours absorb water differently.

As you've seen sourdough starter is highly variable, influenced by factors like flour type and kitchen temperature. This variability is both the challenge and charm of sourdough. Understanding the unique 'character' of your starter is essential for success. You'll need to learn when your starter is hungry, most active, and ready to use.

Don't worry, I will provide all the tools you need to create, maintain, and understand your sourdough starter. Baking, especially sourdough, is about adapting and developing intuition. Your starter has its own rhythm, and the joy of sourdough baking is learning to follow it. With patience and practice, you'll gain the confidence to trust your instincts and adapt, ensuring each loaf reflects your skill and the unique nature of your starter.

EQUIPMENT OF BREAD BAKING

As with any skill, if we really want to achieve remarkable results and avoid failures, frustration, and wasted time, we need to equip ourselves with the right tools—especially in the world of gluten-free sourdough baking. Not everything is necessary from day one, but some tools are indispensable. I've divided the equipment into two categories.

The first category includes essential tools, such as a scale, which are crucial for consistent results. The second category includes tools that enhance quality or ease but are not immediately necessary. Start with the essentials, and if you enjoy the process, consider adding specialized equipment.

The goal of this selection is to keep equipment costs to a minimum, allowing you to invest more in high-quality ingredients. If you don't already have any of the essential equipment listed, you can expect to spend around $70-$90 to get everything you need to start baking successfully.

ESSENTIAL EQUIPMENT

- **Scale Capable of Measuring in Grams (from 10$ to 20$)**

A kitchen scale that measures in grams is essential for baking, especially with gluten-free ingredients. Precision is key, as slight variations can significantly affect the outcome. Measuring by weight ensures consistency, helping achieve the right balance of ingredients every time.

- **Thermometer (from 10 to 25$)**

A digital thermometer is indispensable for monitoring the temperature of water, dough, and your kitchen. Water temperature is key to activating yeast, while the dough's internal temperature indicates when bread is fully baked. Additionally, knowing the temperature of your kitchen is equally important; many recipes suggest using lukewarm water or proofing dough in a warm place, but without knowing the exact temperature, this can be difficult to achieve consistently.

If you opt for a thermometer with a wired probe, you'll also be able to monitor your oven's temperature more accurately. Home ovens often don't match the temperature you set, which can make it tricky to get the perfect bake.

- **Mason Jar (15$ for a pack of 2)**

A 16oz Mason jar is ideal for maintaining your sourdough starter. The clear glass allows easy monitoring of growth, and the wide mouth makes feeding simple. I typically use a 16oz wide mouth jar, which I find to be the optimal size. I recommend having at least two jars: one to hold your starter and another to transfer the amount of starter you'll need for your dough. This way, you keep your main starter clean and intact while preparing your recipes.

- **Glass Mixing Bowls (25$ for a set of 3)**

Glass mixing bowls are versatile and essential for any baker. They allow you to see dough consistency, are non-reactive, retain heat well, and are easy to clean. A set of various sizes will cover all your mixing needs, from small starters to large batches.

- **Silicone or Plastic Bowl/Dough Scraper (5$)**

A silicone or plastic bowl scraper is a simple but invaluable tool in baking. It helps scrape down bowls, prevents waste, and makes handling sticky dough easier. A scraper can help you manage dough with minimal handling, which is especially important for maintaining the structure of gluten-free doughs that lack the elasticity of traditional gluten-based doughs.

ACCESSORY EQUIPMENT

- **Dutch Oven (from 50$ to 70$)**

A Dutch oven is an excellent tool for baking bread as it creates a mini-steam oven effect, which is crucial for developing a beautiful, crispy crust. The heavy lid traps steam released from the dough, promoting oven spring and helping to create the classic crusty exterior of artisan bread. There are two main types of Dutch ovens: enameled and cast iron.

- **Enameled Dutch Oven:** This type has a smooth, non-reactive coating that prevents food from sticking and makes cleaning easier. It also doesn't require seasoning like traditional cast iron. Enameled Dutch ovens are available in various colors and look attractive on the kitchen counter, but they can be more expensive. They are perfect for those who prefer low-maintenance cookware with the added benefit of aesthetics.

- **Cast Iron Dutch Oven:** A traditional cast iron Dutch oven without enamel requires seasoning to maintain its non-stick surface and prevent rust. It is highly durable, retains heat exceptionally well, and often comes at a lower price point than enameled versions. It's ideal for those who enjoy classic, heavy-duty cookware and don't mind the upkeep of maintaining the seasoning. While not absolutely necessary, using a Dutch oven can elevate your bread to the next level, providing a more professional look and texture.

Choosing between enameled or cast iron depends on your personal preference for maintenance and aesthetics. A size that works well in most situations typically ranges from 4 to 5 quarts, offering enough space for a standard loaf while ensuring even heat distribution.

- **Banneton Basket (from 20$ to 30$ for a set of two)**

A banneton basket, also known as a proofing basket, helps shape your dough during the final rise and provides structure, especially for wetter gluten-free doughs. It also leaves a beautiful spiral pattern on the dough, which adds to the artisanal appearance of your bread. In the beginning, using a simple bowl for proofing your loaf can be sufficient, and it's a great way to start without investing in specialized equipment right away. As you gain experience, you might find that a banneton basket offers additional benefits, but it's not a necessity when you're just starting out. A round 8-inch banneton or an oval 9-inch one will work well with the dough quantities in the recipes found in this book.

- **Stand Mixer (from 130$ to 300$)**

A stand mixer can make the process of mixing and kneading dough much easier, especially with the often stickier, more challenging textures of gluten-free doughs. It saves time and effort, allowing for more consistent mixing that's hard to achieve by hand. While you can certainly mix by hand, a stand mixer is a worthwhile investment if you plan on baking frequently, as it can handle heavier doughs and multiple batches.

- **Dough Scoring Razor/Lame (10$)**

A dough scoring razor, or lame, is used to make precise cuts or slashes on the surface of the dough before baking. These cuts control the expansion of the dough, allowing it to rise evenly and creating a beautiful, decorative finish. While a sharp knife can be used, a lame provides better control and cleaner cuts, which is particularly helpful when working with softer gluten-free doughs that can easily deflate with improper scoring.

- **Strainer for Dusting (10$)**

A small strainer is perfect for dusting your work surface, banneton, or the top of your dough with flour. This helps prevent sticking and can also be used for adding a light dusting of flour on the finished loaf for a rustic look. It's a simple tool, but it makes handling the dough much easier and adds a professional touch to your finished bread.

- ### Cooling Rack (8$)

 A cooling rack is useful for properly cooling your bread once it comes out of the oven by allowing air to circulate around it, which helps maintain the desired texture of the crust and prevents the bottom from becoming soggy. However, this tool isn't essential since you can also cool your bread on the oven rack. It becomes particularly helpful if you're baking multiple batches consecutively, as it frees up space and ensures each loaf cools evenly and stays crisp.

- ### Loaf Pan (from 10$ to 20$)

 A loaf pan is great for making sandwich bread and other loaves that require a more defined shape. It supports the dough as it rises, helping to achieve a consistent, uniform loaf ideal for slicing. While you can bake free-form loaves directly on a baking sheet, a loaf pan becomes essential if you decide to make loaf-style bread. In that case, you can choose to purchase a large 2 lb pan or two smaller 1 lb pans. These sizes will work well with the dough quantities in the recipes in this book.

- ### Baking Stone (40$)

 A baking stone, or pizza stone, is used to replicate the intense, even heat of a traditional bread oven. It absorbs moisture and distributes heat evenly, promoting a better rise and a crispier crust. While not essential, a baking stone can significantly enhance the texture of your bread, making it a valuable addition if you're looking to refine your baking results. Personally, I prefer using a Dutch oven for most of my baking, but if you plan on making pizza or focaccia frequently, a baking stone could be a great option for you.

PANTRY ESSENTIALS

In this chapter, we'll dive into a crucial aspect of gluten-free baking: your ingredients. As I've mentioned earlier, investing in high-quality ingredients will yield far better results than splurging on non-essential equipment. The quality of your flours, starches, and other staples directly influences the texture, flavor, and success of your bread.

Gluten provides elasticity and structure in conventional doughs, creating chewiness and allowing the dough to trap air and rise. In gluten-free baking, we rely on blends of flours, starches, and thickeners to replicate these properties, building structure, adding flavor, and achieving the perfect crumb.

TYPES OF FLOUR

Gluten-free flours have distinct flavor profiles and baking characteristics. Some add a light aroma, others bring a bold flavor. Certain flours create a light texture, while others produce a denser crumb. The key to well-balanced bread lies in blending flours to suit your preferences.

In this section, we'll explore the best flours for gluten-free baking. Understanding their properties will help you craft the perfect mix.

Additionally, I'll suggest a commercial mix that I've found to perform reasonably well if you prefer a more convenient option.

- **Rice Flour,** made from finely milled white or brown rice, is a cornerstone of gluten-free baking. Its light, fine texture and neutral flavor make it an ideal base for many gluten-free flour blends. Rice flour helps to create a smooth and soft crumb, essential for achieving a light, airy texture in bread. It lacks the elasticity of gluten but adds bulk and a mild taste that allows other flavors to come through. It's versatile and can be used in a wide range of gluten-free recipes, especially those that aim for a light, airy bread texture.

- **Corn Flour** is made from finely ground cornmeal and brings a distinct, mildly sweet flavor and a golden color to gluten-free breads. It adds a slightly crumbly texture and a touch of corn taste, making it a unique addition to gluten-free flour blends. While it doesn't provide much structure on its own, corn flour enhances the overall flavor profile of baked goods. It's ideal for adding flavor and color to breads, but should not be used as the primary flour due to its crumbly texture

- **Sorghum Flour** is made from an ancient grain that is naturally gluten-free and highly nutritious. It has a mild, slightly sweet flavor with a hint of nuttiness, making it a great addition to gluten-free blends. Sorghum flour adds body and a tender crumb to bread, and its high protein and fiber content contribute to the nutritional value of the finished product. It works well in both light and dense breads, adding depth without overpowering other flavors.

- **Buckwheat Flour,** despite its name, is gluten-free and unrelated to wheat. It has a strong, earthy flavor with a slightly nutty undertone, making it a bold choice in gluten-free baking. Buckwheat flour adds a dark color and hearty taste to breads, making it ideal for rustic loaves. It is also rich in protein, fiber, and essential minerals, enhancing the nutritional profile of your bread. It pairs well with milder flours like rice or sorghum to create a balanced taste. It's particularly suitable for dense, rustic breads where a strong, earthy flavor is desired.

- **Almond Flour** is made from finely ground blanched almonds and is known for its rich, buttery flavor and high-fat content. It adds moisture, tenderness, and a mild sweetness to baked goods, making it a popular choice for enhancing flavor and texture in gluten-free baking. Almond flour also boosts the nutritional value of bread with healthy fats, protein, and fiber. It's best suited for quick breads, muffins, and other baked goods where a tender crumb is desired. Due to its high-fat content, almond flour can also help extend the shelf life of gluten-free breads.

- **Teff Flour** comes from a tiny ancient grain native to Ethiopia and is highly nutritious, rich in protein, iron, and calcium. It has a slightly sweet, earthy flavor with a hint of molasses, adding a unique complexity to gluten-free bread. Teff flour also contributes to a darker color and a denser texture, making it ideal for hearty, robust loaves. It pairs well with lighter flours to balance its density and strong taste, making it a great choice for hearty, flavorful breads.

- **Millet Flour** is made from small, ancient grains and has a mild, slightly sweet, and nutty flavor. It's a good source of protein, fiber, and essential nutrients, adding nutritional value to your gluten-free baking. Millet flour contributes a soft and tender crumb to bread, making it a versatile addition to flour blends. It's suitable for a variety of baked goods, including light loaves and hearty breads.

- **Cassava Flour** is made from the whole root of the cassava plant and is similar to tapioca flour, but with a more neutral flavor and greater versatility. It provides a mild, neutral taste and contributes to a structure and chewiness that helps mimic the properties of gluten. It's versatile and works well in a wide range of baked goods, especially where a more traditional wheat-like texture is desired.

MY TOP BLENDS

These are my favorite flour blends. After much experimentation, these blends consistently give the best results, offering a well-balanced flavor and aroma. For convenience, I prepare these blends in advance and store them in containers, ready to use.

Starches aren't included in these blends because their type and amount vary by recipe. I add them separately when preparing the dough, allowing greater flexibility in fine-tuning texture and structure.

- **Brown Rice and Sorghum:** This blend mixes brown rice flour and sorghum flour in equal parts, and it's my go-to for both its simplicity and excellent results. The mild flavor of brown rice combines with the subtle sweetness of sorghum, creating a balanced profile suitable for various breads. The texture is tender, striking a balance between dense and light, ideal for everyday baking. The hydration is moderate, allowing the dough to absorb water well, making it easy to handle and shape. Overall, this blend is perfect for sandwich loaves and rolls, offering consistent, straightforward results for those new to gluten-free baking.

  Both brown rice and sorghum are also my preferred flours for creating and maintaining a sourdough starter, making them versatile staples in gluten-free baking. Their consistent performance makes them my top recommendation for anyone starting their gluten-free sourdough journey. If you're just beginning, invest in these flours for both your starter and baking.

- **Teff, Sorghum, and Millet Flour Blend (Lectin free):** This blend combines one part teff flour, one part sorghum flour, and half a part millet flour. Teff adds a slightly sweet, earthy flavor with a hint of molasses, sorghum contributes mild sweetness and a tender crumb, and millet adds a light, slightly bitter note, used in smaller amounts for balance.

  For those avoiding rice flours, this blend offers an excellent alternative. It provides a well-rounded texture and complex taste, ideal for darker, rustic and dense breads. If you're looking to keep things even simpler and purchase only two flours, I recommend sorghum and teff. You can create your sourdough starter with sorghum and then use a mix of both flours for your dough, making it an efficient and versatile choice for your baking needs.

- **Buckwheat, White Rice, and Brown Rice Flour Blend:** This blend combines one part buckwheat flour, one part white rice flour, and one part brown rice flour. Buckwheat adds a robust, earthy flavor with nuttiness, while white rice flour provides a light, neutral profile that balances buckwheat's strength and offers a soft crumb. Brown rice flour adds a mild, nutty flavor, structure, and nutritional value.

  This blend is perfect for a balanced bread. The rice flours soften the bold taste of buckwheat, making it ideal for daily use with a less rustic flavor. It provides a pleasant, mildly nutty taste, making it a versatile, dependable all-purpose mix.

What About Commercial Mixes?

Commercial flour mixes are a quick and economical option for making gluten-free bread at home, offering convenience by saving time and effort. However, they often contain binders and starches in undefined quantities, making consistency challenging. This lack of control over the blend's composition can lead to a final product that is overly gummy or inconsistent in texture. Additionally, as we mentioned earlier, these mixes are not suitable for creating your own sourdough starter due to their content of additives.

I must admit that in the past, I frequently used various commercial mixes and brands, experiencing mixed results. Some provided decent outcomes, while others were far from satisfactory. The commercial mix that gave me the most reliable results—and happens to be the most readily available in my area—is the **Measure for Measure Gluten-Free Flour** by King Arthur.

This mix are well-balanced, and it can produce decent results for quick bread-making. If you're looking for convenience and don't have specific sensitivities, this blend can be a reasonable option to have on hand.

STARCHES

Starches play a crucial role in gluten-free baking by helping to achieve the right consistency, structure, and crumb. They mimic gluten properties, providing lightness, binding, and desirable texture. Starches absorb water and gelatinize during baking, trapping air to create a softer, cohesive crumb and improving mouthfeel. The right combination of starches can transform a gritty loaf into one that is tender and enjoyable. Below are some of the most commonly used starches in gluten-free baking, along with their characteristics:

- **Potato Starch (not potato flour),** derived from potatoes, is valued for its high binding properties and ability to add moisture, resulting in a soft, tender crumb. It contributes to a fluffy texture, making it ideal for breads needing more volume and airiness. Its fine consistency helps create a smooth dough, which is why it's often included in various flour blends.

- **Arrowroot Starch,** from the arrowroot plant, is a thickening agent with a neutral flavor and smooth texture, ideal for lightening bread structure. It creates a fine, delicate crumb, perfect for softer breads, and blends well with other starches and flours.

- **Tapioca Starch,** also known as tapioca flour, is extracted from cassava root and adds chewiness and elasticity, mimicking gluten. It aids in browning and crispiness, making it a favorite for those looking to achieve a bread that not only tastes good but also has a pleasing texture and appearance.

- **Cornstarch,** made from corn, is a staple in gluten-free baking for its fine texture and ability to add lightness. It creates a tender crumb and helps stabilize batters, improving softness and texture.

In my recipes, I often use two types of starch to balance texture and performance, resulting in a refined crumb and improved quality. However, you can still achieve good results with just one type of starch if options are limited. The key is to maintain the total amount specified in the recipe. Many people ask if starches can be substituted due to availability issues. Fortunately, starches are generally interchangeable, and you can maintain the same quantities when substituting.

Binders and thickeners are essential for replicating the structure and stability that gluten provides. Without gluten, doughs lack elasticity and binding power, making binders crucial for improving texture, stability, and proper rise.

BINDERS, THICKENERS AND OTHER INGREDIENTS

WHOLE PSYLLIUM HUSK: is a natural fiber and my go-to binder in gluten-free baking. It provides elasticity and structure by forming a gel-like consistency when mixed with water, mimicking gluten's properties. This adds volume, chewiness, and helps create a traditional bread-like texture with a nicer crumb. Whole psyllium husk consistently delivers superior results in both texture and structure.

If whole psyllium husk is unavailable, substitute with psyllium husk powder, using half the amount, as the powder is more concentrated. While both work well, I find whole psyllium husk gives a better crumb and texture, making it my preferred choice.

XANTHAN GUM AND GUAR GUM: are common thickeners in gluten-free products, offering similar benefits in binding and elasticity. Xanthan gum is derived from fermented sugars, while guar gum comes from guar beans and is effective in retaining moisture, preventing dryness. Guar gum offers a slightly different texture and can be used as an alternative or complement to xanthan gum.

You won't find xanthan or guar gum in my recipes, as many people, including my daughter, find that gums can cause digestive discomfort.

HEAT-ACTIVATED BAKING POWDER: Unlike regular baking powder, which activates in two stages—first with moisture and then with heat—this type activates solely during baking. This helps avoid over-proofing and provides a more controlled rise, making it ideal for sourdough bread. While it's not strictly necessary since the sourdough starter does most of the work, heat-activated baking powder can provide extra lift for a lighter, airier crumb, offering valuable support. If you're interested in giving it a try, I recommend "I'm Free Perfect Gluten-Free Baking Powder".

MAPLE SYRUP AND HONEY: are natural sweeteners that enhance the flavor, texture, and moisture of gluten-free breads. Maple syrup adds a warm sweetness with caramel undertones, contributing to browning and a golden crust, while helping keep bread soft. Honey is sweeter with a floral flavor, retaining moisture well and acting as a humectant, extending shelf life. Both are not strictly necessary but can enhance flavor, moisture, and quality, adding natural sweetness and a refined crumb.

EGG WHITES: are mainly water and proteins, which, when incorporated into dough, create a stable structure and add volume. Their proteins provide binding properties that mimic gluten's elasticity, resulting in a lighter, airier crumb and better rise. Egg whites also enhance the bread's appearance, promoting a golden crust. They are particularly beneficial in recipes where a light and fluffy texture is desired.

GLUTEN-FREE STARTER BLUEPRINT

Making a sourdough starter is a time-honored tradition, passed down through generations, and it carries with it a sense of connection to the past. Over the centuries, bakers from all over the world have developed various methods to cultivate this lively mixture of flour, water, wild yeast, and beneficial bacteria.

From now on, accuracy in measuring your ingredients is critical to your success, and that's why we'll be using grams as our unit of measurement. When baking, small differences can have a big impact, and using cups can lead to significant inconsistencies. For example, the weight of 1 cup of flour can range anywhere from about 110 to 130 grams, a variation of nearly 20%. This might not seem like much, but in sourdough baking, where the balance of flour and water is crucial, such discrepancies can affect your starter's performance. Using grams ensures precision, especially during this delicate phase.

Creating your gluten-free sourdough starter is like a new relationship: it requires attention, care, and patience. But it's incredibly rewarding, and soon you'll have a thriving starter uniquely yours, ready to leaven your bread and elevate your baking.

STEP-BY-STEP STARTER GUIDE

Before we dive into the step-by-step guide, let's go over some important details about the equipment you'll need:

- **Kitchen Scale (grams)**
- **Wide-Mouth Glass Jar:** It's a good idea to have more than one 16 ounce glass jar on hand, so you always have a clean one ready for use. A wide mouth makes feeding and stirring easier, while the transparency helps you monitor the starter's progress. Opt for jars with straight, vertical sides to easily track the rise in volume as your starter develops.
- **Cheesecloth or Jar Lid:** You'll need something to cover the jar that allows air to flow while keeping out dust and contaminants. A cheesecloth secured with an elastic band or the jar lid loosely placed on top will work well.
- **Plastic or Wooden Spoon**
- **Silicone Spatula**
- **Bottled or Filtered Water:** The quality of your water matters. Use bottled or filtered water to avoid any chemicals that might be present in tap water, which could hinder the starter's growth.
- **Brown Rice Flour or Sorghum Flour:** I recommend using finely ground flours, preferably organic, for the best results. While you can use any type of whole grain gluten-free flour to create your starter, keep in mind that different flours absorb varying amounts of water, which may require adjustments to the ratios. Sticking with one of the two recommended flours, or a mix of them if you prefer, will allow you to follow the water and flour measurements provided in this guide without any modifications.
- **Rubber Bands:** Use rubber bands to mark the level of your starter in the jar after each feeding. This will help you easily track its growth and activity.

DAY 1

Begin by thoroughly washing the glass container you've chosen to use. There's no need to sterilize it, but make sure it's cleaned well and dried completely. Once your jar is clean, weigh the empty container and write down its weight on a piece of tape that you can stick onto the jar. This will help you keep track of exactly how much starter you have inside as you progress.

Now, add 50 grams of your chosen flour and 50 grams of water to the jar. Aim to use water that's between 75-83°F (24-28°C) to create the ideal environment for the starter to begin fermenting. Stir the mixture thoroughly with a clean spoon until it has the consistency of pancake batter. If you're using sorghum flour, you might need to add a few extra grams of water to achieve the right consistency.

After mixing well, use a silicone spatula to scrape down the sides of the jar, pushing any flour residues back into the mixture. This step is important because it helps prevent any stray bits of dough from drying out and possibly developing mold over time. Cover the jar with a cheesecloth or the jar lid, making sure not to screw the lid on tightly—just rest it on top and give it a slight twist to allow for a gentle airflow. This light air passage is crucial during this early phase.

Finally, place a rubber band around the jar at the level of your mixture (to monitor its growth) and let it sit at 75-83°F (24-28°C) for 24 hours. The location you choose is crucial for the success of your sourdough. Avoid placing your starter near doors or windows, as drafts can slow down the fermentation process. Also, be sure to keep it out of direct sunlight, which can overheat the starter and affect its activity.

DAY 2

After 24 hours, inspect your starter for signs of activity. You might find yourself in one of two different situations:

- You might notice small bubbles forming or a slight rise in the level of the mixture. If you see these early signs of fermentation, give the mixture a good stir, making sure to scrape down the sides and push any residue into the starter. Then wait another 24 hours.

- If you don't see any signs of activity yet, don't worry—this is perfectly normal at this stage. Simply stir the mixture and wait another 24 hours before moving on to Day 3. If, after 48 hours, there are still no visible signs of activity, proceed to the next step anyway.

DAY 3

You should start to notice some bubbles in your sourdough starter, this is a great sign that your starter is active and the natural yeast and bacteria are multiplying. This means it's time to feed your starter. Each time you feed it, you'll want to maintain a ratio of 1:1:1 by weight: equal parts starter, water, and flour.

To keep flour usage to a minimum and avoid unnecessary waste, you'll need to discard a portion of your starter before feeding. During these early days, the discarded starter should not be used in recipes, as it still contains a high level of undesirable bacteria that could be harmful to your health. As the days go by, your starter will become more robust and balanced, with the beneficial yeast and bacteria taking over.

So, start by discarding the topmost layer of the starter and measure out 50 grams. In a clean jar, add the 50 grams of starter, 50 grams of water, and 50 grams of your chosen flour. Mix everything thoroughly, making sure to scrape down the sides so that all the flour is incorporated into the mixture.

Once mixed, clean the sides of the jar with a spatula, cover it loosely with a cheesecloth or lid, and set it back in its warm spot. Your starter is on its way to becoming a thriving culture, so keep an eye on it as it continues to develop.

DAYS 4-10

By now, your starter should be rising consistently, almost doubling in size. If it's not, continue following the Day 3 instructions. You'll need to feed your starter using the 1:1:1 ratio (equal parts starter, flour, and water) whenever it reaches its peak activity. After each feeding, the starter will rise and form a dome on top. Eventually, the rise will slow, and the dome will start to flatten and collapse. So, the ideal time to feed your starter is when the dome loses its shape and becomes flat.

The time it takes for your starter to reach its peak can vary depending on the strength of the starter and the room temperature. The closer you keep it to a temperature of 83°F (28°C), the faster it will ferment. At lower temperatures, like 75°F (24°C), the process will slow down. Over these days, keep an eye on your starter to figure out when it needs feeding. You may need to feed it twice a day.

DOME   **PEAK ACTIVITY**   **COLLAPSED**

Start by discarding the topmost layer of the starter and measure out 50 grams. In a clean jar, add the 50 grams of starter, 50 grams of water, and 50 grams of flour. Stir the mixture thoroughly, scrape down the sides of the jar to prevent any residue from drying out and potentially molding, and cover it loosely with a cheesecloth or lid.

> **Note:** Don't worry about feeding your starter at the exact moment it peaks. As a general rule, it's better to feed it after it has collapsed (but don't wait too many hours, or it may become overly acidic) than to feed it while it still has plenty of flour to "consume."

DAY 11 & BEYOND

At this point, your starter should be ready for baking. To ensure your starter is active, strong, and mature, it should meet the following criteria:

- **Bubbling and Rising:** A mature starter should be consistently bubbly and reach peak activity within 3-6 hours after feeding (this time range depends primarily on the room temperature and the type of flour used).

- **Consistency and Aroma:** The starter should have a thick, airy consistency, similar to a fluffy batter, and a pleasant, slightly tangy aroma. If it smells overly sour, vinegary, or like acetone, it might need more frequent feedings to balance out the bacteria and yeast.

Both conditions should be met for at least 3 consecutive feedings to confirm that your starter is strong and ready for use.

You can also start using the discard in your recipes. Now that your starter is well-established, the discard is no longer full of harmful bacteria and is safe to incorporate into a variety of baked goods.

STARTER CARE AND MAINTENANCE

Once you've created an active and mature starter, you'll need to continue caring for it, much like you would for a living organism. The more attention and care you give to maintaining your starter, the stronger and more balanced it will become over time, improving with each passing week and month.

For optimal care, your starter should be fed whenever it reaches its peak activity, or at most, a few hours after it collapses. To feed your starter, discard the top layer, measure out 50 grams, and use a 1:1:1 ratio (equal parts starter, flour, and water). Always use a clean jar when refreshing your starter.

Then you have two options: keeping it at room temperature or storing it in the refrigerator.

I recommend this option only for those who bake at least 4 or 5 times a week. A starter kept at

ROOM TEMPERATURE MAINTENANCE

room temperature between 72-83°F (22-28°C) requires significant attention and can lead to a lot of flour waste since it needs to be fed about twice a day. To reduce the frequency of feedings, you can use a 1:2:2 ratio (one part starter, two parts flour, two parts water). This gives the starter more "food" to consume, allowing it to last longer before the next feeding. However, during summer, when kitchen temperatures are high, this might not be enough, and you'll need to find a cooler spot or switch to storing the starter in the fridge.

Regardless, when maintaining your starter on the counter, avoid direct sunlight, drafts, or placing it near heat sources like ovens or stovetops, as these can cause temperature fluctuations and affect the consistency of your starter's activity.

Maintaining your starter at room temperature requires daily commitment, but it keeps your starter at its most active and ready to use at a moment's notice. By understanding the signs of peak activity and adjusting for environmental factors, you'll keep your gluten-free sourdough starter healthy, vibrant, and consistently ready for baking.

REFRIGERATION MAINTENANCE

This is the easiest method and the one I recommend if you bake only once or twice a week. By now, after reading the previous pages, you should have a good understanding of how your starter behaves. When kept warm, it becomes more active and quickly consumes its food. When kept cold, it slows down significantly, becoming much "lazier." This means the fermentation process will slow, and you'll be able to feed it less frequently.

So, after doing the usual 1:1:1 feeding, cover the jar loosely with a cheesecloth or lid and leave it at room temperature for 30 minutes (in summer) or 1 hour (in winter). This helps kick-start the fermentation process, giving the yeast and bacteria a chance to activate before the cold slows them down. The next time you need to feed your starter, take it out of the fridge and proceed with the feeding. Just remember to leave it at room temperature for 30 minutes to 1 hour before putting it back in the fridge.

You can keep your starter in the fridge for up to a week before feeding it again. If you forget to feed it after a week, it can generally go up to two weeks without feeding, but it's best to stick to regular feedings to maintain its strength. The longer it goes without feeding, the more the balance between the yeast and bacteria may shift, potentially weakening the starter

Remember, temperature matters here too. Ideally, your fridge should maintain a constant temperature around 40°F (4°C). If, for example, your starter is kept at a slightly warmer temperature, around 47-50°F (8-10°C), the fermentation process will be faster, and it might need a feeding sooner than a week. Additionally, avoid placing the starter near the back or front of the fridge, where temperatures can fluctuate.

LOW-WASTE STARTER MAINTENANCE

It's always disappointing to discard part of your sourdough starter with each feeding—no one likes the idea of wasting ingredients. Fortunately, there are ways to minimize this waste without compromising the health and vitality of your starter.

During the early stages of creating your starter, when it is still particularly delicate, it's essential to maintain at least 100 grams of starter in the jar. Having less than this amount can make your starter more vulnerable to external factors, slowing down its development and making the process more difficult. The higher volume helps create a stable environment where the yeast and bacteria can thrive, leading to a stronger, more resilient starter.

Once you're confident that your starter is mature, active, and strong, you can reduce the amount you keep in the jar, ensuring you maintain at least 40-50g. By doing so, you'll also reduce the amount of flour used for feedings and minimize the discard. This way, you can maintain an efficient routine without wasting ingredients while still keeping your starter healthy and ready for baking.

If you want to eliminate discard altogether, you can align the day you need to feed your starter with the day you plan to bake. This way, you can use the discard directly in your preferment, avoiding waste entirely. All you need to do is keep the right amount of starter in your jar according to the amount used in your recipes.

For example: you can maintain around 80-90 grams of starter in the fridge, which is ideal if you bake once a week. When you're ready to make the preferment, take out the starter and use the amount required for your recipe—typically between 50 and 60 grams.

After you've taken what you need, feed the remaining starter with equal parts flour and water, based on the amount you've used. So, if you've used 60 grams of starter for your recipe, feed the remaining starter with 30 grams of water and 30 grams of flour. Once it's fed, you can put the starter back in the fridge.

LONG-TERM STARTER CARE

When life gets busy or you're heading off on vacation, you may find it difficult to maintain a regular feeding schedule for your sourdough starter. If you know you won't be able to feed it for more than a week, you can adjust your feeding ratio to 1:2:2 or 1:3:3 (starter: flour: water). This will provide enough nutrients to keep your starter healthy for up to 2 weeks. I don't recommend leaving it for longer than that, as the risk of weakening your starter is high, and it will become very acidic. If you expect to be unable to feed your starter for more than 14 days, I suggest using one of the methods listed below to ensure your starter remains healthy.

Drying Your Starter

Drying your starter is one of the best ways to pause its activity for extended periods, and it's a reliable method that can keep your starter safe for months or even years.

Here's how to do it:

1. **Dry the Starter:** Spread a thin layer of active starter on a piece of parchment paper, aiming for an even distribution to speed up the drying process. Allow it to dry completely at room temperature, which usually takes about 24 hours, but can vary depending on humidity levels.

2. **Store the Dried Starter:** Once fully dehydrated and brittle, break the dried starter into small flakes. Place these flakes into an airtight container or a jar, and store it at room temperature away from direct sunlight. Avoid exposing the dried starter to extreme temperatures, and for the best results, refresh it once a year by making a new batch.

3. **Rehydrating the Starter:** To reactivate your dried starter, place the flakes in a jar with warm water and allow them to dissolve. Once dissolved, begin feeding the rehydrated starter with equal parts flour and water until it reaches a thick paste consistency. Continue with the discard and feeding process as you would with a regular starter. It may take about 2 days of feeding before you start seeing signs of activity, such as bubbles and a rise in volume.

Personal Recommendation: I personally recommend drying a portion of your starter once it's well-established and stable. This provides you with an emergency backup in case something goes wrong with your current starter. Having a dried version stored safely ensures that you can easily restart without losing all your hard work.

Freezing Your Starter

Freezing is another useful method for long-term storage, especially if drying isn't an option. While it's generally more challenging to revive a frozen starter compared to a dried one, freezing can still preserve your starter effectively.

1. **Freeze the Starter:** Place a portion of your active starter into an airtight container, leaving some space for expansion. Seal the container tightly and place it in the freezer. For optimal preservation, refresh the frozen starter once a year by starting a new batch.

2. **Thawing and Reviving:** When you're ready to use your frozen starter, transfer it from the freezer to room temperature and allow it to thaw naturally. Avoid using a microwave or any heat source to speed up the thawing process, as this can damage the starter. Once thawed, proceed with the discarding and feeding routine. It will likely take a few days of regular feedings before you start noticing any activity, such as bubbles and a rise in volume, indicating that the starter is coming back to life.

HOW TO USE YOUR DISCARD

When maintaining your sourdough starter, you'll generate discard each time you feed it. For safety, it's important to wait at least two weeks before using the discard in any recipes. During this time, the starter matures and the balance of beneficial bacteria and yeast stabilizes, making the discard safe for consumption.

Once the initial two-week period has passed, you can store your discard in the refrigerator for up to a week. Keep in mind that the longer it remains in the fridge, the more sour its flavor will become, which can add an extra tangy depth to your recipes. After this period, your discard becomes a valuable ingredient that you can use in a variety of creative ways.

Sourdough discard recipes are specially designed to utilize the discard, adding a delicious tangy flavor to dishes without relying on its leavening power. These recipes can range from savory to sweet, turning what might seem like kitchen waste into a key ingredient for new culinary adventures.

Curious about all the delicious possibilities?
Download for free our exclusive bonus eBook dedicated entirely to sourdough discard recipes and discover how to transform this overlooked ingredient into mouthwatering creations.

SCAN THE QR CODE TO GET IT!

COMMON PROBLEMS & SOLUTIONS

Even with careful maintenance, your gluten-free sourdough starter may sometimes face issues. Here's a guide to troubleshooting some of the most common problems and how to address them:

- **Water Layer on Top of the Starter**

A watery layer, known as "hooch," forms on top of the starter. This is usually a sign that your starter is hungry and hasn't been fed often enough.

Pour off the hooch, discard all but 50 grams of the starter, and feed it with 50 grams of flour and 50 grams of water. To prevent this from happening again, if your starter is kept at room temperature, increase the feeding frequency or move it to a cooler spot. If it's refrigerated, ensure you're feeding it at least once a week.

- **Mold**

Mold can develop when the sides of the container aren't cleaned properly after feeding, when using a jar that hasn't been thoroughly cleaned, or when mixing with an unclean utensil. It can also occur if the starter isn't fed for an extended period or if it was created in an overly humid environment.

If the mold is present only on the sides of the jar and not on the starter itself, carefully clean the sides of the container and transfer the starter to a clean jar. Before transferring, make sure to clean the sides thoroughly to reduce the chances of the starter coming into contact with the mold while moving it to the new container. Keep a close watch on the starter in the following days. If mold reappears, unfortunately, it's best to discard the starter and start fresh.

If the mold is present on the starter itself, even in small amounts, there's nothing that can be done to save it, and you'll need to begin with a new batch.

- **I Can't See Any Activity In My Starter**

If your starter isn't showing any signs of bubbling or rising within the first 4 to 5 days, it could indicate that the natural yeast and bacteria are not active, and it may be time to start over. Next time, ensure the temperature is within the optimal range for fermentation, ideally between 75-83°F (24-28°C). If your starter is too cold, it may take longer to become active, so try placing it in a warmer spot in your kitchen.

Another common cause of inactivity could be the use of tap water. In many cities, tap water contains high levels of chlorine, which can be harmful to the beneficial bacteria in your starter. To avoid this, use bottled or filtered water instead. This simple change can significantly improve the chances of your starter becoming active.

- **My Starter Seems to Have Stopped Being Active After a Few Days**

It's not uncommon for your starter to show strong signs of activity at first, only to seemingly slow down or stop after a few days. This can be concerning, but it's actually a normal part of the sourdough starter development process.

During the early days, your starter is beginning to establish a balance between the wild yeast and the bacteria. The initial burst of activity is often due to the presence of bacteria that produce gas quickly, but this phase doesn't last. As the more stable, beneficial yeasts and bacteria take over, the activity can temporarily slow down, giving the impression that the starter has stalled.

Don't worry—this is completely normal. The key is to keep feeding your starter regularly, maintaining a consistent feeding schedule, and keeping it in an environment with a stable temperature. With patience, your starter will regain its strength and become active again as the balance between yeast and bacteria stabilizes.

- **My Starter Isn't Doubling in Size**

It's important to remember that a starter doubling in size isn't the only sign of a healthy and mature culture. The key indicators of an active starter are the bubbles and whether it reaches peak activity. If your starter only increases by 60-70%, that's not necessarily a problem. What's important is that it's growing consistently and reaches peak activity—meaning it's bubbly and full of gas—within 3-6 hours after feeding. As long as your starter is active and showing signs of fermentation, the exact amount of rise is less critical than its overall health and performance.

- **Starter Too Runny or Too Thick**

If your starter's consistency isn't quite right—either too runny or too thick—it can impact its activity and performance in baking. A runny starter often suggests over-fermentation or an imbalance in the water-to-flour ratio, with too much water added. To correct this, adjust by feeding your starter with slightly more flour and a bit less water until it reaches the consistency of a thick pancake batter. Additionally, if over-fermentation is the issue, which can occur in higher temperatures, consider increasing the feeding frequency or ratio to 1:2:2 to stabilize its activity.

On the other hand, if your starter is too thick, it may be dehydrated or not have enough water. To bring it back to the right consistency, add a bit more water during the next feeding until it becomes smooth and slightly runny, similar to a thick batter. Be mindful of the environment, as a very dry atmosphere can contribute to the starter thickening. Adjusting the hydration levels accordingly will help maintain a healthy, active starter that's ready for baking.

- **Pink or Orange Discoloration in Your Starter**

If your starter develops a pink or orange coloration, it's a clear sign that something has gone wrong. This discoloration usually indicates the presence of harmful bacteria or mold, which can occur if the starter has not been fed frequently enough, has been stored in unsanitary conditions, or has been exposed to contaminants. Unfortunately, when your starter turns pink or orange, it's no longer safe to use, and it's best to discard it and start over with a fresh batch.

However, if you're using buckwheat flour, a slight pinkish hue is normal. Buckwheat naturally has pigments that can cause a mild pink or purplish tint in the starter. This color change isn't harmful and doesn't indicate spoilage. To prevent confusion, it's important to know the difference: buckwheat's natural pinkish tint is subtle, whereas harmful bacteria will usually cause a more vivid or unnatural shade of pink or orange.

To avoid problems with spoilage in the future, ensure you are feeding your starter regularly, keeping your jar and utensils clean, and maintaining a stable environment that discourages harmful bacterial growth. Remember, a healthy starter should typically have a creamy off-white or light tan color, with no unusual hues unless you're working with specific flours like buckwheat.

- **Can I Feed My Starter with a Different Type of Flour?**

While your starter is still developing and not yet strong and active, it's important to feed it consistently with the same type of flour. Changing flours too early can cause the starter to become unstable or slow down its activity. Once you're confident that your starter is active, strong, and mature, there won't be any issues with using a different type of flour for the feedings. However, it's important not to switch flours too frequently to avoid weakening your starter.

Constantly changing the type of flour can weaken your starter, making it less vigorous.

If you need to use a different type of flour due to availability or other reasons, continue using the new flour for the next feedings to give the starter time to adjust and maintain its strength.

- **My Kitchen Is Too Cold**

If your kitchen is too cold, your starter may not ferment as actively as it should. A cold environment slows down the natural yeast and bacteria, which can result in a sluggish or inactive starter. There are a few ways to provide a warmer environment:

- **Find a Warmer Spot in Your Home:** Check if there's a place in your home that's slightly warmer than your kitchen, such as near a radiator or in a cupboard close to a heat source. Just make sure the spot is not too hot, as temperatures above 83°F (28°C) can overstimulate the starter.

- **Use the Oven with the Light On:** One effective trick is to place your starter in the oven with the light on. The warmth from the oven light creates a cozy, consistent environment for fermentation. However, make sure to attach a note to the oven's control panel reminding you to remove the starter before turning on the oven. This simple step can prevent accidental baking of your starter!

- **Use a Proofing Box or Yogurt Maker:** If you have a proofing box or a yogurt maker with adjustable temperature settings, you can use these to keep your starter at an optimal temperature. Set the temperature between 75-83°F (24-28°C) to help your starter thrive.

- **Hot Water Bottle:** You can also fill bottles or other containers with hot water and place them near your starter to create a warmer environment. Just make sure the heat is gentle and not too hot, as excessive heat can damage the starter.

- **I Forgot My Starter In The Fridge For Too Long Without Feeding It**

If you've forgotten about your starter in the fridge for a long time, or if you notice that it has become weak, you can revive it by performing frequent small feedings. This method involves giving the starter smaller amounts of food more often, which increases the proportion of bacteria and yeast compared to the flour, allowing them to digest it more quickly and regain strength.

Here's how to proceed: take 50g of your starter, add 25g of flour and 25g of water, and leave it at 75-83°F (24-28°C). Once the starter reaches its peak activity, repeat the process using the same ratio. Continue these frequent feedings until your starter consistently reaches peak activity within 3-6 hours after each feeding. This will help restore its vitality and strength.

In this chapter, we'll explore everything you need to know to create the perfect dough. From understanding how to properly mix ingredients to achieving the right consistency, you'll be guided through every step.

Before we dive into the details of mixing and kneading, it's important to understand one crucial aspect of sourdough baking: it involves many variables, and results may not always be perfect on the first try. Factors like temperature, humidity, the flour you use, and the activity level of your sourdough starter can all affect the outcome.

Over the next few pages, I'll provide you with as many tips and tricks as possible to help you navigate these variables, but it's important to recognize that we can't account for every single factor. Don't get discouraged if your first loaf isn't flawless. With time, as your experience grows, you'll become more attuned to the specific needs of your dough and discover what works best in your kitchen.

But here's the good news: gluten-free baking offers a significant advantage over traditional wheat-based baking. When working with gluten, bakers need to use specific kneading techniques to develop a strong gluten structure, which can be time-consuming and tricky. In gluten-free sourdough baking, however, there's no need for those complex methods. Your goal is simply to mix the ingredients until they're evenly combined, creating a smooth and homogeneous dough.

So while sourdough baking can have its challenges, the process of working with gluten-free dough is much simpler. With patience and practice, you're already well on your way to mastering this rewarding skill!

STEP 1: ENSURE THAT YOUR STARTER IS ACTIVE AND HAPPY

Before you start working on your dough, it's essential to ensure that your starter is active and strong. A weak or inactive starter won't be able to create the light, airy, and flavorful bread you're aiming for. Follow these simple guidelines to make sure your starter is in top condition:

- **If you haven't fed your starter in the last 5-7 days,** you will need to feed it before using it to build the preferment. Simply take it out of the fridge and feed it in a 1:1:1 ratio (equal parts starter, water, and flour). After feeding, you have two options to follow:

  1. Let the starter sit at room temperature for 30 minutes to an hour before placing it back in the fridge. You can then proceed with the preferment after 24 hours.

  2. Leave the portion of the starter needed for the recipe at room temperature until it reaches its peak (usually 3-6 hours depending on the temperature and strength of the starter), and proceed to Step 2. Store the remaining starter in the fridge for future use, after allowing it to sit at room temperature for 30 minutes to 1 hour.

  However, don't be fooled by a collapsed starter. After reaching its peak, your starter will eventually stall and then begin to deflate. You can tell if your starter has collapsed by looking for a dry line around the jar, typically at the point where it had doubled in size. This is a sign that the starter reached its peak and then collapsed. In this case, you can still proceed with the preferment but don't wait too long.

- **If you have fed your starter within the last 5-7 days,** it is likely strong and ready to go. You can skip this step and proceed directly to build the preferment.

> **Note:** *If you fed your starter 24 hours ago and stored it in the fridge, make sure it has reached its peak activity before using it. If it hasn't, leave it at room temperature until it does, then proceed with the preferment.*

STEP 2: PREPARING THE PREFERMENT

The preferment, also known as the levain, is what will make your bread rise, giving it a light and airy texture. Essentially, it's a portion of your active starter mixed with water and flour, similar to a regular feeding. The preferment also imparts the sour flavor that's so distinctive in sourdough bread. For this reason, I prefer to create the preferment using a 1:2:2 ratio. This allows the preferment to mature over a longer period, enhancing the sourness in the final loaf.

Another advantage of using the 1:2:2 ratio is that it lets you keep a smaller amount of starter in the fridge. For example, to make 250g of mature preferment, you only need 50g of active starter.

How to prepare the preferment:

- Ensure that your starter is active and happy (refer to Step 1 for guidance).
- Take the necessary amount of active starter for your recipe, and remember to always save some for future use. Never use all of your starter to make the preferment!
- Add water and flour. For example, if the recipe calls for 50 g of active starter, add 100g of flour and 100g of water. Mix until smooth.
- Cover loosely and let the preferment at room temperature until it reaches its peak, typically 6-10 hours (if you're using starter directly from the fridge, the preferment will reach its peak more slowly.) While it's not crucial to use the preferment exactly at its peak activity, don't wait too long, or its leavening power will start to decrease.

Especially for your first few attempts, use a container with straight, narrow sides for your preferment. This makes it easier to monitor its growth and accurately identify when it reaches peak activity.

Tips: If you want a more sour flavor, increase the fermentation time by leaving the preferment at a cooler temperature (68-72°F or 20-22°C). For a less sour taste, ferment for less time at a warmer temperature (79-83°F or 26-28°C).

> **Note:** *When creating your preferment, feel free to use different flours, such as the same flour mix used in the recipe. This rule applies only to the preferment. The starter, however, should be fed as consistently as possible with the same type of flour.*

STEP 3: MIXING AND SHAPING THE DOUGH

Before we dive into the details, it's important to remember that achieving the right dough consistency is key to a successful gluten-free sourdough loaf. This step will be divided into two main parts: first, we'll focus on mixing the ingredients to create a cohesive and well-hydrated dough. Then, we'll move on to shaping the dough to ensure it's ready for proofing and baking.

MIXING THE INGREDIENTS

Mixing the ingredients correctly is a crucial step in creating a successful gluten-free dough. It involves combining wet and dry ingredients to form a cohesive and well-hydrated mixture that will serve as the base of your bread. In this section, we will break down the process into clear, manageable steps to ensure you achieve the perfect dough consistency.

1. **Weighing and Preparing the Ingredients:** It's important to weigh and prepare all your ingredients in advance. This helps avoid any mistakes caused by rushing and ensures you won't forget to include any crucial components.

2. **Preparing the Psyllium Gel:** Whisk together the psyllium husk and water vigorously for 30-60 seconds until it is fully incorporated. Let the mixture rest for about 5-10 minutes to fully hydrate and reach a gel-like texture.

3. **Mixing Dry Ingredients:** Meanwhile, in a large bowl or stand mixer, combine the flours, starches, sea salt, and any other dry ingredients. Ensure these ingredients are thoroughly mixed to ensure even distribution.

4. **Mixing Wet Ingredients:** Once the gel has formed, add the ripe preferment and any other wet ingredients, like olive oil or sweeteners if using. Mix until everything is well combined and smooth.

5. **Combining Wet and Dry Mixtures:** Add the psyllium-preferment gel mixture to the dry ingredients. If using a stand mixer with a dough hook or mixing by hand with a large spoon or spatula, start combining the two until they begin to form a dough. Make sure to knead the dough until it is smooth and all ingredients are fully incorporated. This typically takes about 5-10 minutes.

The goal is to mix just until all the ingredients are fully combined and no dry flour remains visible. The dough should be cohesive, soft, and slightly sticky but should still hold together without being overly wet or runny. A good rule of thumb is to stop mixing as soon as the dough has reached a uniform consistency. If using a mixer, keep it on a low speed and check frequently to avoid over-mixing. If mixing by hand, use a gentle folding motion rather than vigorous stirring, which can overwork the dough.

One of the key challenges is avoiding overworking the dough. Since gluten-free doughs lack the gluten network, they can easily become overworked, resulting in a dense, gummy texture.

Testing Dough Consistency

To determine if your dough has the right consistency, you can use the following practical tests:

- **The Visual Check:**

Look for a Thick, Shaggy Texture: The dough should appear rough and slightly shaggy, not smooth or overly shiny. It should be wet enough to hold together but not so wet that it resembles a runny batter.

- **The Touch Test:**

Soft and Slightly Sticky: When you touch the dough, it should feel tacky but not unmanageable. A little stickiness is good; it means there's enough moisture to support fermentation and rising. Pliable, Not Rigid: The dough should be pliable, bending easily without cracking. If it feels too firm or dry, add a small amount of liquid and mix again.

- **The Spoon or Spatula Test:**

Trail and Spread: Scoop some dough with a spoon or spatula and let it slide off. It should slowly fall off and spread slightly on the surface. If it clumps together or falls off in chunks, it's likely too dry. If it drips too quickly like a batter, it's too wet.

- **Adjusting Consistency On the Fly:**
  - **Too Dry:** Gradually add more liquid, a tablespoon at a time, until the dough softens to the desired consistency.
  - **Too Wet:** Add more flour, one tablespoon at a time, mixing well after each addition, until the dough is just firm enough to hold its shape without spreading excessively.

SHAPING THE DOUGH

This is an essential step that helps give your bread its final form, ensuring an even rise and a well-structured crumb. Here, we'll walk you through the main stages of shaping, providing you with guidance on how to handle the dough confidently and effectively. Once all the ingredients are fully incorporated into the dough, transfer it to a lightly floured or lightly oiled work surface and follow this simple steps:

1. **Flatten the Dough:** Gently press the dough into a disc using your hands.

2. **Fold the Top Edge:** Take the top edge of the dough and fold it towards the center, pressing gently to seal.

3. **Fold the Bottom Edge:** Fold the bottom edge up towards the center, overlapping the previous fold. Press gently to seal the layers together.

4. **Fold the Sides:** Fold the left side of the dough towards the center, followed by the right side, just like folding a letter.

5. **Shape into a Round Ball:** Carefully flip the dough over so the seam is facing down. Use your hands to gently shape the dough into a round ball by tucking the edges underneath and rotating it on the work surface. This step helps create a smooth surface and adds tension to the outer layer of the dough. If you want to create an oval shape, instead of stopping at the ball, gently roll the dough back and forth from the top, stretching it slightly until you achieve the desired oval shape.

6. **Final Shaping:** Cup your hands around the dough and gently rotate it on the work surface to create a tight, smooth ball. Continue shaping until the surface is taut, but be careful not to overwork the dough.

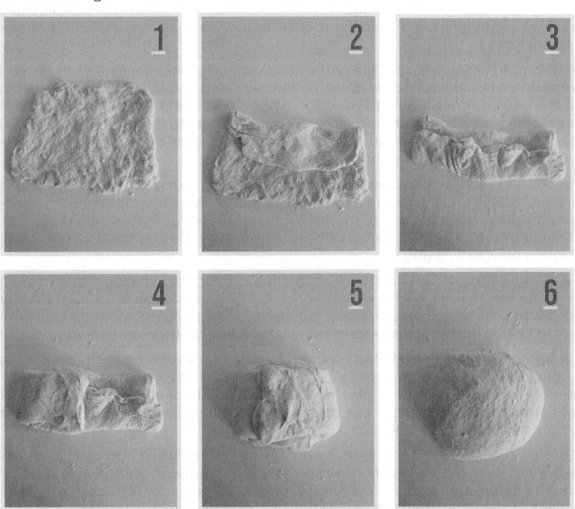

Once you've shaped your dough, the next step is to place it in a proofing basket to help maintain its shape during the final rise. The size and preparation of your proofing basket are crucial to ensure your bread develops a strong, stable structure.

1. **Choosing the Right Proofing Basket:** The size of the proofing basket is very important. Using a basket that's too large can cause your dough to spread out and flatten, while the correct size will support the dough, helping it maintain a strong and stable shape as it proofs. For the recipes in this book, an 8-inch round or 9-inch oval banneton works perfectly. Alternatively, you can use a 2.5 qt glass mixing bowl as an effective substitute.

2. **Preparing the Proofing Basket:**

   - If you're using a banneton, make sure to dust it generously with flour before placing the dough inside. This prevents the dough from sticking and helps retain the shape during proofing.

   - If you're using a glass mixing bowl, line it with a clean kitchen towel and then sprinkle it with flour. This setup provides a similar non-stick surface and structure, ensuring your dough maintains its form.

3. **Transferring the Dough:** Use a dough scraper to lift it gently from the work surface. The dough should be placed upside down in the basket—meaning the side that was facing down on the work surface should now face up.

Tips for Handling Sticky Dough

Gluten-free doughs are notoriously sticky, and managing this stickiness is key to a smooth baking process. Unlike traditional doughs, gluten-free doughs rely on a blend of flours, starches, and binders that often result in a much tackier texture. This can make handling, shaping, and transferring the dough a challenge if you're not prepared. However, with the right techniques and a few practical tips, you can effectively manage stickiness and work with your gluten-free dough with confidence.

- Use Water or Oil on Your Hands: One of the simplest and most effective methods for handling sticky dough is to keep your hands damp or lightly coated with oil. Water acts as a barrier, preventing the dough from clinging to your skin, while a thin layer of oil, such as olive or vegetable oil, can provide a slick surface that makes the dough easier to handle. Simply dip your fingers in a bowl of water or rub a small amount of oil onto your palms before working with the dough. Reapply as needed to maintain a barrier against stickiness.

- Use Wet or Oiled Utensils: Just as with your hands, keeping your mixing tools, spatulas, or dough scrapers wet or lightly oiled can help manage stickiness. When dividing or transferring dough, dip your utensils in water or coat them with a bit of oil to reduce friction and prevent the dough from sticking. This technique is particularly useful when portioning dough into rolls or transferring it from a bowl to a baking pan.

- Chill the Dough: If the dough is too sticky to handle comfortably, chilling it in the refrigerator for 15-30 minutes can make a significant difference. Cooling the dough firms it up slightly, making it less tacky and easier to shape. This step is especially helpful for recipes that call for shaping or braiding, as chilled dough holds its form better and is less prone to spreading.

- Use Parchment Paper or Silicone Mats: When shaping or transferring sticky dough, working on a piece of parchment paper or a silicone baking mat can be a game-changer. These surfaces are non-stick and allow you to handle the dough without it adhering to your work surface. Parchment paper can also be used to line baking pans, making cleanup easier and preventing the dough from sticking during baking.

- Work Quickly: The longer you handle sticky dough, the more likely it is to stick to your hands and surfaces. Try to work quickly and confidently, shaping the dough with deliberate motions. The less time the dough spends in contact with your hands, the better it will behave. This approach helps maintain the dough's structure and prevents unnecessary frustration.

STEP 4: PROOFING AND RISING

Proofing, the process of allowing dough to rest and rise before baking, is another crucial step in bread-making. Unlike traditional dough, gluten-free dough won't double in size; instead, it typically increases by about 50-70%. This more subtle rise is perfectly normal, as gluten-free dough doesn't trap gas in the same way as wheat-based dough.

Once your dough is shaped and placed in the proofing basket, you can choose one of the following methods based on your schedule and preference:

- **Room Temperature Proofing:**

Cover the proofing basket with a damp tea towel and leave it to proof in a warm place for several hours. Typically, this takes about 3-5 hours, depending on the ambient temperature. Warmer temperatures will speed up proofing, while cooler temperatures will slow it down.

- **Cold Proofing (Overnight in the Refrigerator):**

Alternatively, you can proof the shaped dough in the refrigerator for 8-12 hours, which allows you to bake fresh bread in the morning. Before refrigerating, cover the proofing basket with a damp tea towel or plastic wrap to prevent it from drying out. Then, let the dough rise at a temperature ideally between 75°F and 82°F (24°C and 28°C) for about 1 hour to kick-start the fermentation process. After this initial rise, place the dough in the refrigerator. Cold proofing helps develop deeper flavor and offers a more flexible baking schedule. If you notice that the dough is drying out too much in the fridge, consider placing the entire basket inside a reusable plastic bag for extra protection. If the dough has reached the right level of proofing, you can bake it straight from the fridge without needing additional time to warm up.

FACTORS THAT INFLUENCE PROOFING TIME

Proofing gluten-free dough requires attention to several key factors that can significantly influence how long the process will take. Understanding these variables can help you adjust your proofing time for the best results, whether you're doing a bulk fermentation or a final proof.

When it comes to bread baking, proofing times are highly variable, and with sourdough, even more so. In the recipes in this book, the proofing times provided are simply guidelines. As you'll see, there are several factors that can affect these times, such as the environment and the nature of your sourdough starter. Don't rely too much on the exact times; instead, carefully observe how your dough is rising in your specific conditions and with your starter, adjusting the proofing times accordingly. This approach will allow you to fine-tune the process and replicate successful results in future bakes.

Let's explore these factors in more detail:

1. **The Health and Activity of Your Starter:** The strength of your sourdough starter greatly affects proofing time. An active, well-fed starter will ferment the dough faster, while a sluggish or unfed starter will slow the process. Incorporating the starter at its peak activity ensures a smoother and more predictable proofing.

2. **Room Temperature:** The temperature in your kitchen directly influences proofing speed. Warmer environments (75-80°F or 24-27°C) accelerate fermentation, while cooler temperatures (below 70°F or 21°C) slow it down. In colder kitchens, consider using a proofing box or the oven with the light on to maintain a warmer environment.

3. **Refrigerator Temperature**: Not all refrigerators are set to the same temperature, which can greatly affect proofing times. Cooler settings slow down fermentation, while warmer spots, like the top shelves (which can be up to 10°F/5°C warmer), speed it up. Adjusting where you place your dough helps control the proofing process effectively.

4. **Hydration Level of the Dough:** The water content (hydration) in your dough affects proofing time. Higher hydration doughs ferment faster but are harder to handle, while lower hydration doughs rise more slowly. Adjusting hydration helps control both fermentation speed and the bread's final texture.

5. **The Type of Flour Used:** Different gluten-free flours proof at varying rates. For example, rice flour ferments faster than denser flours like sorghum or buckwheat. Starch-heavy blends proof quickly but can collapse if over-proofed. Adjust proofing time based on your flour mix's ability to absorb moisture and support fermentation.

6. **The Ratio of Starter to Flour:** The amount of starter you use relative to the amount of flour in your dough impacts how fast the dough will proof. A higher ratio of starter to flour introduces more active yeast and bacteria, which speeds up fermentation. For example, if your dough contains a high percentage of starter (say 30-50% of the flour weight), it will proof faster than a dough with a lower percentage (10-20%). If you're using a smaller amount of starter, expect the dough to take longer to rise, which can be useful if you're looking to develop more complex flavors over a longer fermentation.

7. **Your Altitude:** If you live at a higher altitude (above 3,000 feet or 900 meters), you'll notice that fermentation tends to happen more quickly. This is because there is less air pressure, allowing the gases produced by fermentation to expand more rapidly. The lower air pressure also means dough can rise faster and may over-proof more easily. In high-altitude environments, it's important to monitor your dough closely and potentially shorten proofing times to avoid over-proofing. Additionally, you may need to slightly adjust hydration levels to account for the drier air, which can affect moisture retention in your dough.

VISUAL AND TACTILE INDICATORS OF READINESS

In bread-making, whether with gluten or gluten-free, one of the most crucial aspects is knowing when your dough is ready to bake. It's essential to avoid baking too early (underproofed) or too late (overproofed).

In gluten-free baking, this becomes even more important, as gluten-free dough transitions quickly from underproofed to overproofed compared to traditional dough. To help you master this delicate balance, here are some tips:

1. **Look for Surface Changes:** One of the first signs that your gluten-free dough is proofing correctly is the appearance of small bubbles or a slightly aerated surface. These bubbles are an indicator of active fermentation and show that your starter is doing its job. While gluten-free dough doesn't double in size like wheat-based dough, you should notice a slight puffiness and a relaxed look to the surface. This puffiness indicates that gases are building up inside the dough, but it's important that the dough doesn't become overly expanded, which could lead to overproofing.

2. **The Poke Test:** The poke test is a simple but effective way to assess whether your dough is ready for the oven. Gently press the surface of the dough with your fingertip, creating a small indentation.

   Then, observe how the dough reacts:

   - **If the indentation slowly fills back in halfway,** the dough is perfectly proofed and ready to bake. This indicates that the dough has developed enough gas to rise but still has enough strength to maintain its structure during baking.

   - **If the indentation springs back quickly,** the dough needs more time to proof. In this case, the dough hasn't developed enough gas and needs further fermentation to reach the right level of activity.

   - **If the indentation doesn't fill back at all and the dough deflates,** it's a sign that the dough may be overproofed. Overproofed dough has expanded beyond its structural capacity, making it fragile and more likely to collapse during baking.

You might find that dough proofed in the fridge won't expand as much and tends to feel firmer, making it harder to determine if it's ready to bake. For your first attempt, try baking the dough after the shortest recommended proofing time, then adjust as you gain experience. If you're cold-proofing, it's often best to bake the dough straight from the fridge once you believe it has reached the right level of proofing, as allowing it to warm up too much can lead to overproofing and negatively impact the final texture.

As with all stages of bread-making, mastering the proofing process comes with time and experience. While it may be challenging at first to recognize the subtle signs of a perfectly proofed loaf, each attempt will refine your skills and intuition. With patience and practice, you'll gain the confidence and expertise needed to consistently judge when your dough is ready for the oven.

> **Note:** Remember that your oven needs about an hour to fully preheat. To prevent overproofing, start preheating well before your dough reaches its peak. This way, your oven will be ready at the perfect moment, ensuring your dough transitions smoothly into the baking stage.

STEP 5: SCORING

This is a process that is often underestimated. Many people believe that scoring is purely for aesthetic purposes, but in reality, it plays a critical role in the baking process.

Scoring creates weak points in the dough's surface, directing where it will expand during baking. This gives you control over the bread's final shape, ensuring a more uniform rise. Additionally, scoring contributes to the development of an open crumb structure. By allowing the dough to expand along the cuts, you promote the formation of air pockets, which are key to achieving that light and airy crumb that so many bakers aim for.

Without scoring, the bread can burst or tear at random points, leading to an uneven shape and texture.

And, of course, scoring is an opportunity to get creative! Beautiful scoring designs not only make your bread more visually appealing but also give it a signature look.

How to Score Your Dough

Before scoring your dough, make sure your oven has reached the proper baking temperature. This ensures that as soon as you've scored the dough, it can go directly into the oven without losing any structure.

When your dough is ready, carefully turn it out from the proofing basket onto a piece of baking paper.

If you'd like to make your scoring more pronounced, you can dust the dough lightly with fresh flour using a small fine-meshed sieve.

Be sure to use a very sharp blade. Dip the blade in water to prevent the dough from sticking, making it easier to achieve clean and precise cuts. Scoring should be done with confident, swift motions. Aim for cuts that are between ¼ and ½ inch (6 mm to 10 mm) deep. Hesitating or moving too slowly can cause the dough to stick to the blade, resulting in uneven cuts or tears in the dough. By making quick, smooth cuts, you'll help ensure the dough expands properly in the oven and creates the desired pattern.

Tips

- **Chill the Dough Before Scoring:** Cold dough is much easier to score, as it holds its shape better. If you've proofed your dough at room temperature, consider chilling it in the refrigerator for about 30 minutes before baking. This firming-up period makes the dough more manageable and helps create cleaner cuts.

- **Vary the Angle of Your Blade:** Adjusting the angle of your blade can produce different effects. A shallow angle will create wider openings, while a steeper angle results in finer, more delicate lines. You can experiment with these angles to achieve the look you desire.

- **Bake Immediately After Scoring:** Once you've scored your dough, it's important to get it into the oven right away. If the dough sits too long after scoring, it will begin to deflate and lose some of its structure, leading to a less successful rise.

You've come this far. After carefully nurturing your starter, mixing and proofing your dough with patience and precision, you're now at the final and perhaps most rewarding stage of the process. Baking your bread is the moment where everything comes together—the rich aroma that fills your kitchen, the crackling crust that forms as the dough rises, and the satisfaction of seeing the transformation unfold before your eyes.

But the magic doesn't end when the bread comes out of the oven. Knowing how to cool your bread properly is just as important as the bake itself, preserving the delicate structure you've worked so hard to achieve. And then there's the question of how to store it, ensuring that every slice remains fresh and flavorful for as long as possible.

In this chapter, we'll guide you through the final steps that turn your dough into something truly special. From the precise moment it hits the oven, to letting it cool on the rack, and finally storing it so you can enjoy it over the coming days. These moments are where your hard work becomes something you can savor and share with others.

BAKING

One often overlooked but fundamental step in baking is preheating. Before discussing the techniques, it's essential to understand why preheating is so important. Proper preheating ensures that the oven reaches the ideal temperature, creating the perfect environment for your bread to achieve the right texture, rise, and structure—especially crucial in gluten-free baking.

Since gluten-free dough lacks the elastic structure provided by gluten, it needs immediate heat to set its shape and expand evenly. A well-preheated oven ensures that the baking process starts right away, allowing the dough to rise properly and develop a stable structure.

Achieving a thick, crispy crust is one of the hallmarks of sourdough bread, and it's even more important for gluten-free sourdough because the crust provides stability to a more delicate loaf.

Here's how a properly preheated oven benefits your bread:

- **Early crust formation:** A fully heated oven ensures that the dough is exposed to immediate, intense heat, helping to create a defined, crispy crust. If the oven isn't fully preheated, the dough may rise slowly in a warming environment, resulting in a softer crust.

- **Steam generation:** High heat generates steam at the start of the bake, allowing the outer layer of the bread to stretch before forming a crust. This process helps develop a beautiful, golden crust that adds both flavor and structural integrity.

Failing to preheat the oven can lead to several problems:

- **Uneven baking:** Without a consistent heat source, gluten-free dough may rise unevenly, resulting in an irregular crumb structure and inconsistent texture.

- **Dense or gummy interior:** If the oven isn't hot enough, the inside of the bread may remain undercooked, leading to a dense, gummy texture. Gluten-free bread needs immediate heat to evaporate excess moisture and firm up the dough.

- **Inconsistent browning:** An under-preheated oven will cause patchy browning and a less appealing crust, affecting both the appearance and taste of your bread.

To get the best results from your gluten-free sourdough bake, follow these preheating guidelines:

1. **Preheat the oven with your baking vessel:** Preheat your oven for about 1 hour before placing

the bread inside, and make sure to put your baking vessel (such as a dutch oven, baking stone or oven tray) inside from the start. This ensures the vessel reaches the same temperature as the oven, providing an extra boost of heat that aids in the initial rise and helps create a crisper crust. Avoid using the convection (fan) setting, as it tends to dry out the steam and the bread more quickly, which can negatively affect the texture and moisture of your loaf.

2. **Use an oven thermometer:** It's important to double-check that your oven reaches the set temperature, as some thermostats, especially in older ovens, can be inaccurate. An oven thermometer will help you confirm that the oven has reached and maintains the correct temperature, ensuring your gluten-free bread bakes properly.

STEAM IN BAKING: TECHNIQUES AND BENEFITS

Introducing steam during the baking process plays a crucial role in developing the crust and overall texture of sourdough bread. Gluten-free bread can struggle to form the kind of crisp, golden crust typically found in traditional wheat-based loaves, but steam is a game-changer that helps bridge this gap. Understanding how and why to use steam in baking can significantly improve your results, giving your gluten-free sourdough the ideal balance of a crisp exterior and a soft, moist crumb.

Why Steam is Important in Baking

When dough is first placed in the oven, it undergoes rapid expansion due to the heat—a process known as "oven spring." For this to happen efficiently, the outer surface of the dough must remain moist and pliable. This is where steam becomes crucial:

- **Prevents premature crust formation:** Without steam, the crust can harden too quickly, limiting the dough's ability to expand and resulting in a denser loaf. Steam keeps the surface of the dough moist during the critical early stages of baking, allowing the dough to rise to its full potential before the crust sets.

- **Promotes a crispy crust:** As the steam gradually evaporates, it helps the starches on the surface of the dough gelatinize, which is what leads to that beautifully glossy, crispy crust. In gluten-free bread, achieving this type of crust is more challenging because of the lack of gluten's elastic properties, but steam can greatly enhance the final texture.

- **Enhances color and flavor:** The moist environment created by steam also aids in the Maillard reaction, the chemical process that causes browning and caramelization. This contributes to the rich, golden color of the crust and develops deeper, more complex flavors in the bread.

Techniques for Creating Steam at Home

There are several ways to introduce steam into your home oven, even if you don't have a steam-injected oven like those found in commercial bakeries. Below are some effective techniques for creating steam, whether you're using a Dutch oven, a baking stone, or even an oven tray.

1. **Using a Dutch Oven:** Dutch oven is an excellent tool for naturally trapping steam during baking. The tight-fitting lid creates a sealed environment that captures moisture released by the dough, essentially generating steam within the pot. This process mimics the conditions of a professional steam oven, which is why a Dutch oven is often favored for sourdough baking. When you transfer the dough into the hot pot and cover it, the heat and moisture from the dough will immediately create steam.

2. **Water Pan Method:** If you don't have a Dutch oven, you can still create steam using a simple yet effective method: the water pan technique. To do this, as you preheat your oven, place a shallow metal or cast iron pan on the bottom rack. Once the oven is ready and you're about to

place your dough inside, carefully pour a cup of boiling water into the pan. The rising steam keeps the dough moist during the first minutes of baking, helping it expand fully before the crust forms.

For an even more sustained release of steam, you can add a handful of ice cubes to the water pan. As the ice melts slowly, it continues to create steam, giving your dough extra time to rise properly before the crust sets.

It's important to resist the temptation to open the oven door too often while the bread is baking. Every time the door opens, valuable steam escapes, reducing its ability to help the dough rise and form a beautiful crust. Keep the door closed to maintain the steam and ensure the best possible results for your gluten-free sourdough.

Regardless of which technique you use, steam is most beneficial during the first 20-25 minutes of baking, when the dough is still expanding and forming its shape. After this stage, the crust begins to set, and continued steam can prevent it from developing properly. If you're using a Dutch oven, remove the lid after this period. For other methods, you can take out the water pan or simply allow the steam to dissipate naturally by not adding more water.

SIGNS OF A PERFECTLY BAKED LOAF

Knowing when your bread is perfectly baked requires tuning into both visual and sensory cues. Since gluten-free bread doesn't always behave like wheat-based bread, relying on your senses can guide you toward that perfect loaf.

Visual Cues

One of the first things to watch for is the color of the crust. A perfectly baked gluten-free sourdough loaf should have a deep golden-brown or even a light amber color. The browning is a sign that the Maillard reaction has occurred, indicating that the crust is properly caramelized and flavorful. Be aware that different flours can affect the final color.

For example:

- Rice flour-based breads often result in a lighter, more golden color.
- Buckwheat, teff, or millet flours might produce a darker crust due to their natural pigments.
- Sweet or starch-heavy blends can give a more pronounced golden hue due to higher sugar content caramelizing during baking.

Another visual cue is the appearance of small cracks in the crust, which indicates that the bread has expanded fully during oven spring. The surface should look slightly glossy if steam was used effectively during baking, as this indicates the starches have properly gelatinized.

Sensory Cues

One of the best-known methods for checking if bread is done is the "hollow tap" test. Once your loaf has baked for the recommended time, remove it from the oven and tap the bottom of the loaf lightly with your fingers or knuckles. A fully baked loaf should produce a hollow sound, indicating that the interior is fully cooked and the crumb is properly set. If the sound is dull or muffled, it might need a few more minutes in the oven.

A perfectly baked bread should have a firm, crisp crust that resists pressure. If the crust feels soft or gives way easily, it may still be underbaked or could soften too much after cooling.

A lighter loaf suggests that the internal moisture has evaporated properly, leaving you with a well-risen, airy crumb. An underbaked loaf will feel heavy due to retained moisture inside.

Internal Temperature

For a more precise measurement of doneness, you can use a thermometer to check the internal temperature of the loaf.

Insert a probe into the thickest part of the bread:

190°F to 200°F (88°C to 93°C) is the ideal internal temperature range for gluten-free sourdough. At this temperature, the bread is fully cooked through and will have set properly, avoiding the gummy or doughy texture often associated with underbaked gluten-free bread.

If your loaf registers below 190°F, put it back in the oven for an additional 5-10 minutes, checking frequently to ensure the crust doesn't overbake.

MANAGING MULTIPLE BAKES

There are times when you might find yourself needing to increase the amount of bread you're baking, whether for a family gathering or to have a stock of homemade bread on hand. At first glance, the simplest solution might seem to be doubling or increasing the dough size and making larger loaves. However, this approach is more difficult to manage than it appears. A larger loaf demands several adjustments, including changes to baking and fermentation times, oven temperature, proofing basket size, and sometimes even the need for a larger Dutch oven. Moreover, larger loaves often face challenges in developing correctly, which can lead to uneven baking or an undercooked interior.

Instead of making larger loaves, a more effective approach is to bake multiple standard-sized loaves. By doubling the ingredient quantities, you can knead the dough together in one go and then divide it into two or more equal portions. This approach offers greater control over the baking and fermentation process, making it easier to manage without the challenges of a single, oversized loaf. It also provides flexibility, allowing you to bake at your convenience, whether spreading out the baking over the course of a day or across multiple days. As an added benefit, smaller loaves bake more evenly, ensuring a perfect crust and well-developed crumb in each loaf.

When dividing your dough into multiple portions, you have two main options for managing the proofing process, ensuring that each loaf proofs correctly and avoiding the risk of over-proofing.

1. **Room-Temperature Proofing:** Allow one loaf to fully proof at room temperature and bake it as usual. For the second loaf, place it in the fridge just before it reaches its peak. This will slow down the fermentation, allowing you to bake it later, once the first loaf is finished. This approach helps prevent over-proofing and ensures both loaves are baked at the right time.

2. **Cold Proofing:** If you've opted for the slower fermentation method, you'll have two or more loaves resting in the fridge. In this case, simply take out one loaf at a time when you're ready to bake.

COOLING

Cooling your bread is a critical step in the baking process. Just as important as the mixing, proofing, and baking phases, proper cooling ensures that the bread's internal structure sets fully and the flavors develop to their fullest potential.

At the end of baking, the bread is still undergoing important internal changes. The residual heat within the loaf continues to cook and stabilize the crumb structure. If sliced too soon, while the bread is still hot or warm, the crumb can collapse, resulting in a dense or gummy texture. Allowing the bread to cool fully gives the crumb time to firm up, creating a more stable and well-formed interior.

During baking, moisture moves from the center of the loaf to the surface, where it evaporates. Cooling the bread properly allows this moisture to redistribute throughout the loaf, preventing the bread from drying out and ensuring that both the crumb and crust have the right texture. This redistribution is essential for maintaining a soft interior and a crust that isn't too tough or overly dry. Cutting the bread too early causes moisture to escape too quickly, leaving the bread dry and compromising its structure.

In addition to improving texture, cooling also allows the bread's flavor to fully develop. As the bread rests, the residual heat helps break down the remaining starches and sugars, enhancing the depth and complexity of the flavors, particularly in sourdough breads where the fermentation process plays a significant role. By giving the bread time to cool, you not only preserve its structure but also maximize its taste.

The best method for cooling your bread is to transfer it to a wire rack as soon as it's out of the oven. A wire rack allows air to circulate freely around the entire loaf, preventing the bottom from becoming soggy due to trapped moisture. This method promotes even cooling and is ideal for maintaining the integrity of both the crumb and the crust.

How long you let your bread cool depends on the size and type of loaf, but generally, gluten-free sourdough should be allowed to cool for at least 2 hours. This time allows the crumb to set properly and the moisture to redistribute throughout the loaf. Here's a more specific guide:

Resisting the temptation to slice into your bread early is difficult, but essential. Cutting into it too soon can ruin the texture, releasing too much steam and moisture, leaving you with a dense, gummy center that could have been avoided with patience.

STORING

Proper storage is key to maintaining the freshness and texture of your sourdough bread. Because gluten-free bread lacks the natural elasticity and moisture retention properties of gluten, it can dry out or become stale faster than traditional bread. That's why knowing how to store it correctly is essential to ensuring your bread stays soft and delicious for as long as possible. In this section, we'll cover the best practices for short-term and long-term storage, as well as tips for reviving bread that has been stored for several days.

SHORT-TERM STORAGE: KEEPING BREAD FRESH FOR A FEW DAYS

When you plan to eat your bread within a day or two, the goal is to maintain the bread's natural moisture without allowing the crust to become too soft. The best options for short-term storage include wrapping the bread in a clean cloth or placing it in a paper bag. These materials allow just enough airflow to prevent the crust from becoming soggy, while also protecting the crumb from losing too much moisture. If you don't have a paper bag or cloth, you can use a bread box—it provides the right balance of air circulation and protection from the environment.

Avoid using plastic wrap or sealing the bread in a plastic bag for short-term storage, as this traps moisture and softens the crust, leaving it rubbery. While the crumb might stay soft, the crust will lose its texture, which is especially disappointing if you've worked hard to develop a good, crispy crust during baking.

If you're storing sliced bread, it's best to keep the loaf intact and slice only what you need when you're ready to eat it. Exposing the cut surface to air will dry out the bread faster, so keeping the loaf whole as long as possible helps retain moisture.

LONG-TERM STORAGE: FREEZING

If you've baked a large loaf or have extra bread that you won't eat within a few days, freezing is the best option for long-term storage. Gluten-free sourdough bread freezes exceptionally well, retaining much of its original texture and flavor when stored properly. The key to freezing is to minimize moisture loss and prevent freezer burn, which can damage the crumb and make the bread taste stale.

Before freezing, make sure the bread has completely cooled to room temperature. Freezing warm bread can cause condensation inside the packaging, which leads to sogginess when the bread is thawed. Once the bread is fully cooled, wrap it tightly in plastic wrap or aluminum foil, ensuring that no part of the loaf is exposed to air. For extra protection, you can place the wrapped bread in a freezer-safe bag or an airtight container.

For convenience, you might want to freeze the bread in individual slices or smaller portions, so you can thaw only what you need without defrosting the entire loaf. To freeze slices, wrap each slice separately in plastic wrap or parchment paper, and then store them together in a freezer bag. This way, you can grab a slice or two for toast or sandwiches without wasting the rest of the loaf.

Gluten-free sourdough bread can be stored in the freezer for up to three months without losing significant quality. Beyond that time, the texture may begin to degrade, and freezer burn can occur.

THAWING AND REVIVING STORED BREAD

If you've stored a whole loaf, it's best to let it thaw at room temperature. Remove the bread from the freezer, but leave it in its wrapping until fully thawed—this helps prevent moisture from evaporating too quickly. Once the bread has thawed, you can unwrap it and let it sit on a wire rack for a few minutes to allow the crust to regain some of its crispness.

For slices, you can place them directly in a toaster or a preheated oven to both thaw and re-crisp the bread. This method is particularly useful if you prefer warm toast or if the bread feels slightly dry after freezing.

To revive an entire loaf or larger portion of bread, you can refresh it in the oven. Preheat your oven to 350°F (175°C), and place the thawed bread directly on the oven rack. Bake for about 10 minutes, or until the crust becomes crisp and the bread is warmed through. This method restores much of the bread's original texture, giving the crust a nice crunch while keeping the crumb soft and moist. Be cautious not to leave the bread in the oven for too long, as this can cause the crumb to dry out further.

COMMON PROBLEMS & SOLUTIONS

So, you followed the recipe exactly, but the bread didn't turn out quite like you imagined. Maybe it's too dense, too dry, or it just... doesn't look right. Whatever it is, it's not what you signed up for. What went wrong?

Before you point fingers at the recipe, let's take a deep breath and step back. Gluten-free bread baking is an adventure filled with twists and turns. There are many moving parts—some within your control and others, well, not so much. It's not always about doing something wrong; sometimes, it's about understanding what's at play behind the scenes.

Here's the thing: not all ingredients are created equal. You might be using the same brand of flour every time, but the next bag you buy could behave slightly differently. Maybe this batch is ground a little finer, or it's holding a bit more moisture than the last. The protein content might have changed ever so slightly. These invisible factors can nudge your dough in unexpected directions.

Then, there's the wild card: your kitchen. The temperature, humidity, even the altitude—none of these stay constant. Maybe it's a hot summer day and your dough decides to rise faster than you anticipated. Or maybe the extra humidity is turning your dough sticky. And if you're living in a high-altitude area? Well, you're in a whole different ballgame. Dough can act up in ways you'd never expect, all thanks to where you're baking.

But don't throw in the towel just yet! Instead of scrapping everything and starting over, let's troubleshoot. Real progress happens when you learn how to decode these little hiccups. In this chapter, we'll walk through some of the most common gluten-free bread mishaps and—more importantly—how to fix them. Let's turn those flops into triumphs, one loaf at a time.

DOUGH IS TOO STICKY OR DIFFICULT TO HANDLE

Why it happens:

High moisture content and insufficient hydration balance: Gluten-free doughs generally have more moisture than traditional doughs, which is essential for achieving the correct texture once baked. However, the ratio of water to flour may be too high, or the type of flour being used might require less water than expected, leading to an overly sticky dough that's hard to manage.

How to solve it:

- **Adjust hydration levels:** Reduce the liquid in the recipe slightly, but be cautious not to overdo it—gluten-free doughs need moisture. Reduce by a tablespoon at a time and observe the dough's texture.
- **Refer to the tips on handling sticky dough.**

DOUGH DOESN'T HOLD ITS SHAPE

Why it happens:

In traditional doughs, gluten provides the necessary structure. In gluten-free doughs, binders like psyllium husk, xanthan gum, or chia seeds are needed to replicate that structure. When these binders are missing or insufficient, combined with too much liquid in the dough, it will spread and flatten rather than hold its shape.

How to solve it:

- **Add structure-building binders:** Ensure you're using enough binders like psyllium husk, xanthan gum, or flaxseed meal to strengthen the dough. Add an extra teaspoon if necessary and knead well to incorporate it evenly.
- **Reduce hydration:** Slightly reduce the liquid to help the dough hold together better. Reduce it by a tablespoon at a time and observe how the texture changes.
- **Avoid over-proofing:** Keep proofing times shorter, as gluten-free doughs over-proof quickly. Monitor the dough carefully to avoid it becoming too soft.

MY BREAD COLLAPSES

Why it happens:

One of the most common reasons for bread collapsing is over-proofing. If the dough rises for too long, the yeast exhausts its energy, weakening the structure and preventing it from holding the gas bubbles, leading to a collapse. Additionally, baking at a temperature that's too low can prevent the crust from setting properly, making it difficult for the loaf to maintain its shape. Oven temperature fluctuations during baking can also disrupt the process and contribute to the collapse.

How to solve it:

- **Watch the proofing time:** Keep proofing times short and check the dough regularly to avoid over-proofing. Gluten-free doughs can over-proof faster than traditional doughs, so err on the side of caution.
- **Reduce hydration:** If the dough is too wet, slightly reduce the amount of liquid in the recipe. Start by reducing it a tablespoon at a time and see if this helps the dough hold its shape better.
- **Ensure consistent baking temperature:** Preheat your oven properly and avoid opening the door too often during baking. Use an oven thermometer to ensure the temperature remains steady.

BREAD IS TOO DENSE, COMPACT CRUMB

Why it happens:

If the dough doesn't rise enough, it won't develop the air pockets necessary for a light texture. This can be due to weak or inactive starter or under-proofing, where the dough hasn't risen long enough. Additionally, gluten-free doughs require proper mixing to distribute ingredients and incorporate air. Under-mixing can result in a dense loaf, while over-mixing can cause the dough to collapse and lose structure, leading to heaviness.

How to solve it:

- **Check starter activity:** Make sure your sourdough starter is fully active and bubbly before using it in the dough. Feed it several hours before baking, and check for signs of readiness, such as a strong rise, bubbles, and a tangy aroma. An underactive starter won't provide enough leavening power.
- **Mix properly:** Ensure that your dough is mixed thoroughly to incorporate air but avoid over-mixing, which can collapse the structure. A good rule of thumb is to mix until all ingredients are well combined and smooth.
- **Proof properly:** Give the dough enough time to rise, but don't over-proof. It should increase in size but not double like traditional gluten doughs. Keep an eye on it and test the dough for readiness with a gentle finger poke—if it springs back slowly, it's ready to bake.

BREAD IS TOO DRY

Why it happens:

Gluten-free doughs require more moisture than traditional wheat doughs. If the dough doesn't contain enough liquid, the bread will turn out dry. Additionally, over-baking or baking at too high a temperature can further dry out the bread, as gluten-free bread has more difficulty retaining moisture during the baking process.

How to solve it:

- **Increase hydration:** Slightly increase the amount of liquid in the dough by adding water or other liquids (like milk or oil). Start by adding a tablespoon at a time until the dough is sufficiently moist.
- **Avoid over-baking:** Check the bread earlier than the suggested baking time, and ensure you're baking at the correct temperature. You can use a thermometer to check the internal temperature of the bread—around 205°F (96°C) is ideal for gluten-free bread.

BREAD DOESN'T RISE

Why it happens:

If your sourdough starter isn't active or well-fed, it won't produce the gas needed for the bread to rise. Additionally, gluten-free doughs often require more time to proof than traditional doughs. If not given enough time to ferment in a warm environment, the dough won't rise properly. Cold temperatures slow down yeast activity, further preventing the dough from expanding.

How to solve it:

- **Ensure an active starter:** Make sure your sourdough starter is fully active and bubbly before incorporating it into the dough. Feed the starter several hours before baking and check for signs of readiness, such as bubbles, a strong rise, and a tangy aroma.
- **Allow for enough proofing time:** Be patient and allow the dough plenty of time to rise. Gluten-free doughs often take longer to ferment than wheat-based doughs, so give it the time it needs. Keep an eye on the dough, looking for bubbles and a slight spring-back when pressed gently.
- **Control proofing temperature:** Create a warm, draft-free environment for proofing. Ideal temperatures range between 75°F and 82°F (24°C to 28°C). If your kitchen is cold, consider proofing the dough in a turned-off oven with the light on, or using a proofing box.

BREAD CRUMBLES EASILY

Why it happens:

Baking the bread for too long can dry it out, making it more prone to crumbling. Additionally, some gluten-free flours, such as rice or almond flour, can lead to a crumbly texture if not properly balanced with other flours or starches that provide elasticity and structure.

How to solve it:

- **Avoid overbaking:** Keep a close eye on the bread as it bakes and remove it from the oven as soon as it's done. You can check for doneness using a thermometer—the internal temperature should be around 205°F (96°C) for gluten-free bread.

- **Use a balanced flour blend:** Ensure that your gluten-free flour blend contains a good mix of flours and starches. Flours like tapioca or arrowroot help create a more elastic dough, while whole-grain flours like sorghum or brown rice flour add structure.

GUMMY BOTTOMS, GUMMY TEXTURE

Why it happens:

A gummy texture and soggy bottoms often result from a combination of under-baking, excessive moisture, and improper cooling. If the bread isn't baked long enough or at a high enough temperature, the interior remains too wet. Additionally, an overly hydrated dough or cutting the bread too soon after baking can trap moisture inside, leading to a gummy, dense texture.

How to solve it:

- **Increase baking time or temperature:** Make sure the bread is fully baked by extending the baking time or increasing the oven temperature slightly. Use an oven thermometer to ensure the oven is at the correct temperature, and check the internal temperature of the bread (205°F / 96°C is ideal).
- **Reduce hydration:** Slightly reduce the liquid in the dough to avoid an overly wet, gummy crumb. Add liquid gradually and monitor the dough's texture.
- **Allow sufficient cooling time:** Let the bread cool completely before slicing, as gluten-free bread needs time to set and allow moisture to escape. This will help avoid a gummy texture.

LARGE, UNEVEN HOLES IN THE CRUMB

Why it happens:

Large, uneven holes in the crumb are often caused by a combination of over-proofing, improper handling, and inconsistent mixing. Over-proofing allows the dough to expand too much, creating large gas pockets. Additionally, rough or uneven handling during shaping can disrupt the distribution of air bubbles, while inconsistent mixing can lead to uneven gas formation throughout the dough.

How to solve it:

- **Avoid over-proofing:** Keep a close eye on proofing times and stop when the dough has risen sufficiently but not too much. Look for signs of readiness, such as the dough rising to the appropriate level and showing small, even bubbles.
- **Handle the dough gently and consistently:** When shaping the dough, be sure to handle it gently and evenly to avoid disrupting the air bubbles or creating large gaps.
- **Ensure proper mixing:** Mix the dough thoroughly to ensure even ingredient distribution. This helps create a more consistent crumb structure with smaller, evenly spaced holes.

CRUST IS TOO HARD OR BURNT

Why it happens:

A hard or burnt crust is often caused by over-baking, incorrect oven temperature, or a lack of steam during baking. When bread is baked too long or at too high a temperature, the crust can become dry, tough, or even burnt. Additionally, without enough moisture in the oven, the crust may form too thickly, resulting in a hard exterior. Uneven heat distribution in the oven can also lead to parts of the crust burning while other areas remain under-baked.

How to solve it:

- **Reduce baking time and temperature:** After the first 20-25 minutes of cooking, lower the temperature by 50-100°F or shorten the baking time to prevent the crust from hardening. Start checking the bread for doneness earlier than the recipe suggests, and use an oven thermometer to ensure consistent heat.

- **Increase steam during baking:** To create a softer crust, increase the steam by keeping the lid on your Dutch oven for a longer period, or add extra water to the tray on the bottom rack for the first 20-25 minutes of baking.

- **Cover the bread with foil:** If you notice the crust is becoming too hard or starting to burn, cover the bread loosely with aluminum foil during baking.

CRUST IS TOO PALE

Why it happens:

A pale crust is typically the result of incorrect oven temperature, uneven heat distribution, or overproofing. If the oven temperature is too low, the crust won't brown properly and will remain pale. Additionally, if the dough is overproofed, the natural sugars in the dough can be depleted, which inhibits the Maillard reaction responsible for browning.

How to solve it:

- **Ensure accurate oven temperature:** Use an oven thermometer to check that the oven is reaching the correct temperature. If the crust is too pale, increase the temperature slightly or extend the baking time.

- **Rotate the bread for even baking:** To combat uneven heat distribution, rotate the bread halfway through the baking process. This helps ensure that all sides brown evenly, resulting in a consistently golden crust.

- **Avoid overproofing:** Keep a close eye on your dough during proofing to prevent it from overproofing, ensuring there are enough sugars left to support the Maillard reaction for a beautifully browned crust.

BOTTOM OF BREAD IS GETTING EXTRA BROWN OR BURNT

Why it happens:

This issue typically occurs when the direct heat from the oven surface or Dutch oven transfers too much heat to the bottom of the bread, causing it to brown excessively or burn before the rest of the loaf is properly baked. Uneven oven heat can also contribute to the problem.

How to solve it:

- **Use a barrier in the Dutch oven:** Placing a couple of foil rings at the bottom of your Dutch oven can elevate the bread slightly, creating a buffer that reduces direct heat transfer to the bottom of the loaf. Another effective barrier is a silicone bread sling, which provides a non-stick surface and acts as an insulator, reducing the direct heat impact on the bottom of the bread. It also makes it easier to lift the bread out of the Dutch oven once baking is complete.

- **Lower oven temperature:** If the bottom is browning too quickly, try lowering the oven temperature slightly and extending the baking time. This will ensure the entire loaf bakes evenly without the bottom burning.

- **Place the Dutch oven on a baking sheet:** Positioning your Dutch oven on a baking sheet can help by deflecting some of the direct heat from the oven floor, resulting in a more evenly browned bottom.

RECIPES

Welcome to the heart of our gluten-free sourdough journey—this chapter is all about the recipes that will guide your baking experience. Here, you'll find a reliable foundation to help you create a wide variety of gluten-free breads. Keep in mind, though, that baking is both a science and an art. Following the recipes closely is important, as each ingredient plays a specific role, and even small changes can have a noticeable impact on the final result.

It's also worth remembering that proofing and baking times can vary depending on your home environment. Factors like temperature, humidity, and altitude all affect how your dough behaves. Don't be discouraged if your dough takes more or less time to rise, or if the baking time needs adjusting. Trusting your instincts and adapting to the unique conditions of your kitchen is part of the learning process.

As discussed in the Baking, Cooling, and Storing chapter, if you're planning to bake more bread, it's often better to double the ingredients and make two smaller loaves rather than a single larger one. This approach ensures more consistent results and gives you greater control over the baking process. Take your time, enjoy the process, and most of all, have fun experimenting with these recipes!

> **Note:** All of the recipes in the Classic Breads and Special Breads sections can be baked using a 2 lb loaf pan. To do this, simply follow steps 5 and 6, along with the baking method described in the Sandwich Bread recipe on page 53.

Baking Schedule

To help guide you through the process, I've created a sample baking schedule based on my own experience. This schedule outlines the steps and timings that I personally find convenient based on my daily routine and the specific conditions of my kitchen. Feel free to adjust the schedule to suit your lifestyle and kitchen environment.

Warm Proof Schedule

TIME	STEP
9:00 pm	Make preferment in 1:2:2 feeding ratio
6:45 am	Prepare and weigh all the ingredients
7:00 am	Mix & shape the dough, proof at 75-83°F (24-28°C)
10:30 am	Preheat the oven
11.30 am	Bake, then cool for at least 2 hours

Cold Proof Schedule

TIME	STEP
11:00 am	Make preferment in 1:2:2 feeding ratio
7:45 pm	Prepare and weigh all the ingredients
8:00 pm	Mix & shape the dough, proof at 75-83°F (24-28°C)
8:30 pm	Place in the fridge
8.30 am	Preheat the oven
9:30 pm	Bake, then cool for at least 2 hours

SINGLE FLOUR RECIPE

In this selection of recipes, you'll find how it's possible to make great bread with just a few ingredients, focusing on one type of flour at a time. While the results are excellent, with bold flavors and aromas characteristic of whole grain bread, it's important to note that these loaves won't reach the same complexity or lightness as breads made with a blend of different flours and starches.

These recipes are perfect for those who love the hearty taste of whole grain bread or for those looking to experiment before investing in a broader range of ingredients.

Each recipe still offers a unique and satisfying experience, thanks to the versatility of sourdough.

WHOLE MILLET BREAD

Yield: 1 boule

For the preferment
- 50 grams active gluten-free sourdough starter
- 100 grams millet flour
- 100 grams warm water (75-83°F / 24-28°C)

For the dough
- 25 grams whole psyllium husk
- 440 grams water
- 12 grams sugar or honey
- 330 grams millet flour
- 10 grams salt

Nutritional Information (per 100g)

Calories	175
Carbohydrates	34g
Protein	4g
Fat	2g
Fiber	5g

Prepare the preferment

1. In a bowl, mix 50g of active gluten-free sourdough starter, 100g millet flour, and 100g warm water. Gradually add the water to achieve a thick paste-like consistency.
2. Cover the bowl loosely and let the preferment sit at room temperature for 6-10 hours, or until it reaches its peak.

Prepare the dough

3. When the preferment is ready, prepare the psyllium gel. In a medium bowl, vigorously whisk the psyllium husk with water for 30-60 seconds until fully incorporated. Let the mixture sit for about 5-10 minutes to fully hydrate and develop a gel-like texture.
4. In a large bowl or stand mixer, whisk together millet flour and salt. Ensure these ingredients are thoroughly mixed for even distribution.
5. Add the preferment and the sugar or honey to the psyllium gel. Mix thoroughly by hand, with a wooden spoon, or using an electric mixer until the mixture is smooth and well combined.
6. Add the psyllium-preferment gel mixture to the dry ingredients. If using a stand mixer with a dough hook or mixing by hand with a large spoon or spatula, start combining the ingredients until a dough begins to form. Knead the dough until it is smooth and all ingredients are fully incorporated.

7. Transfer the dough to a lightly floured surface and flatten it. Fold the sides of the dough over itself, flip it over, and shape it into a ball or oval depending on your proofing basket. Place the dough upside down in the banneton or in a bowl lined with a kitchen towel if you're not using a banneton. Cover the dough with a tea towel and let it proof for 3-5 hours, or until it is well-risen.

Bake

8. About 1 hour before baking preheat the oven to 450°F (235°C), with the Dutch oven, baking stone, or oven tray inside. If you're not using a Dutch oven, place a shallow metal pan at the bottom of the oven.
9. Gently invert the dough from the proofing basket onto a sheet of parchment paper and score the top. Then, using the edges of the parchment paper, carefully transfer the dough into the preheated vessel (Dutch oven, baking stone, or oven tray) and bake. If you're not using a Dutch oven, pour a cup of boiling water into the shallow pan at the bottom of the oven.
10. After about 25 minutes, remove the water pan or the lid of the Dutch oven, and continue baking for another 40-45 minutes. Once the bread is fully baked, take it out of the oven and let it cool for at least 2 hours before slicing.

WHOLE BROWN RICE BREAD

Calories	190
Carbohydrates	37g
Protein	3g
Fat	2g
Fiber	4g

Yield: 1 boule

For the preferment
- 50 grams active gluten-free sourdough starter
- 100 grams brown rice flour
- 100 grams warm water (75-83°F / 24-28°C)

For the dough
- 25 grams whole psyllium husk
- 330 grams water
- 12 grams sugar or honey
- 270 grams brown rice flour
- 10 grams salt

Prepare the preferment

1. In a bowl, mix 50g of active gluten-free sourdough starter, 100g brown rice flour, and 100g warm water. Gradually add the water to achieve a thick paste-like consistency.
2. Cover the bowl loosely and let the preferment sit at room temperature for 6-10 hours, or until it reaches its peak.

Prepare the dough

3. When the preferment is ready, prepare the psyllium gel. In a medium bowl, vigorously whisk the psyllium husk with water for 30-60 seconds until fully incorporated. Let the mixture sit for about 5-10 minutes to fully hydrate and develop a gel-like texture.
4. In a large bowl or stand mixer, whisk together brown rice flour and salt. Ensure these ingredients are thoroughly mixed for even distribution.
5. Add the preferment and the sugar or honey to the psyllium gel. Mix thoroughly by hand, with a wooden spoon, or using an electric mixer until the mixture is smooth and well combined.
6. Add the psyllium-preferment gel mixture to the dry ingredients. If using a stand mixer with a dough hook or mixing by hand with a large spoon or spatula, start combining the ingredients until a dough begins to form. Knead the dough until it is smooth and all ingredients are fully incorporated.
7. Transfer the dough to a lightly floured surface and flatten it. Fold the sides of the dough over itself, flip it over, and shape it into a ball or oval depending on your proofing basket. Place the dough upside down in the banneton or in a bowl lined with a kitchen towel if you're not using a banneton. Cover the dough with a tea towel and let it proof for 3-5 hours, or until it is well-risen.

Bake

8. About 1 hour before baking preheat the oven to 450°F (235°C), with the Dutch oven, baking stone, or oven tray inside. If you're not using a Dutch oven, place a shallow metal pan at the bottom of the oven.
9. Gently invert the dough from the proofing basket onto a sheet of parchment paper and score the top. Then, using the edges of the parchment paper, carefully transfer the dough into the preheated vessel (Dutch oven, baking stone, or oven tray) and bake. If you're not using a Dutch oven, pour a cup of boiling water into the shallow pan at the bottom of the oven.
10. After about 25 minutes, remove the water pan or the lid of the Dutch oven, and continue baking for another 40-45 minutes. Once the bread is fully baked, take it out of the oven and let it cool for at least 2 hours before slicing.

WHOLE SORGHUM BREAD

Nutritional Information (per 100g)

Yield: 1 boule

For the preferment
- 50 grams active gluten-free sourdough starter
- 100 grams sorghum flour
- 100 grams warm water (75-83°F / 24-28°C)

For the dough
- 23 grams whole psyllium husk
- 410 grams water
- 12 grams sugar or honey
- 280 grams brown rice flour
- 10 grams salt

Calories	180
Carbohydrates	36g
Protein	3g
Fat	2g
Fiber	4g

Prepare the preferment

1. In a bowl, mix 50g of active gluten-free sourdough starter, 100g sorghum flour, and 100g warm water. Gradually add the water to achieve a thick paste-like consistency.
2. Cover the bowl loosely and let the preferment sit at room temperature for 6-10 hours, or until it reaches its peak.

Prepare the dough

3. When the preferment is ready, prepare the psyllium gel. In a medium bowl, vigorously whisk the psyllium husk with water for 30-60 seconds until fully incorporated. Let the mixture sit for about 5-10 minutes to fully hydrate and develop a gel-like texture.
4. In a large bowl or stand mixer, whisk together sorghum flour and salt. Ensure these ingredients are thoroughly mixed for even distribution.
5. Add the preferment and the sugar or honey to the psyllium gel. Mix thoroughly by hand, with a wooden spoon, or using an electric mixer until the mixture is smooth and well combined.
6. Add the psyllium-preferment gel mixture to the dry ingredients. If using a stand mixer with a dough hook or mixing by hand with a large spoon or spatula, start combining the ingredients until a dough begins to form. Knead the dough until it is smooth and all ingredients are fully incorporated.

7. Transfer the dough to a lightly floured surface and flatten it. Fold the sides of the dough over itself, flip it over, and shape it into a ball or oval depending on your proofing basket. Place the dough upside down in the banneton or in a bowl lined with a kitchen towel if you're not using a banneton. Cover the dough with a tea towel and let it proof for 3-5 hours, or until it is well-risen.

Bake

8. About 1 hour before baking preheat the oven to 450°F (235°C), with the Dutch oven, baking stone, or oven tray inside. If you're not using a Dutch oven, place a shallow metal pan at the bottom of the oven.
9. Gently invert the dough from the proofing basket onto a sheet of parchment paper and score the top. Then, using the edges of the parchment paper, carefully transfer the dough into the preheated vessel (Dutch oven, baking stone, or oven tray) and bake. If you're not using a Dutch oven, pour a cup of boiling water into the shallow pan at the bottom of the oven.
10. After about 25 minutes, remove the water pan or the lid of the Dutch oven, and continue baking for another 40-45 minutes. Once the bread is fully baked, take it out of the oven and let it cool for at least 2 hours before slicing.

WHOLE TEFF BREAD

Calories	185
Carbohydrates	34g
Protein	4g
Fat	2g
Fiber	5g

Yield: 1 boule

For the preferment
- 50 grams active gluten-free sourdough starter
- 100 grams teff flour
- 100 grams warm water (75-83°F / 24-28°C)

For the dough
- 20 grams whole psyllium husk
- 380 grams water
- 10 grams sugar or honey
- 300 grams brown rice flour
- 10 grams salt

Prepare the preferment

1. In a bowl, mix 50g of active gluten-free sourdough starter, 100g teff flour, and 100g warm water. Gradually add the water to achieve a thick paste-like consistency.
2. Cover the bowl loosely and let the preferment sit at room temperature for 6-10 hours, or until it reaches its peak.

Prepare the dough

3. When the preferment is ready, prepare the psyllium gel. In a medium bowl, vigorously whisk the psyllium husk with water for 30-60 seconds until fully incorporated. Let the mixture sit for about 5-10 minutes to fully hydrate and develop a gel-like texture.
4. In a large bowl or stand mixer, whisk together teff flour and salt. Ensure these ingredients are thoroughly mixed for even distribution.
5. Add the preferment and the sugar or honey to the psyllium gel. Mix thoroughly by hand, with a wooden spoon, or using an electric mixer until the mixture is smooth and well combined.
6. Add the psyllium-preferment gel mixture to the dry ingredients. If using a stand mixer with a dough hook or mixing by hand with a large spoon or spatula, start combining the ingredients until a dough begins to form. Knead the dough until it is smooth and all ingredients are fully incorporated.
7. Transfer the dough to a lightly floured surface and flatten it. Fold the sides of the dough over itself, flip it over, and shape it into a ball or oval depending on your proofing basket. Place the dough upside down in the banneton or in a bowl lined with a kitchen towel if you're not using a banneton. Cover the dough with a tea towel and let it proof for 3-5 hours, or until it is well-risen.

Bake

8. About 1 hour before baking preheat the oven to 450°F (235°C), with the Dutch oven, baking stone, or oven tray inside. If you're not using a Dutch oven, place a shallow metal pan at the bottom of the oven.
9. Gently invert the dough from the proofing basket onto a sheet of parchment paper and score the top. Then, using the edges of the parchment paper, carefully transfer the dough into the preheated vessel (Dutch oven, baking stone, or oven tray) and bake. If you're not using a Dutch oven, pour a cup of boiling water into the shallow pan at the bottom of the oven.
10. After about 25 minutes, remove the water pan or the lid of the Dutch oven, and continue baking for another 40-45 minutes. Once the bread is fully baked, take it out of the oven and let it cool for at least 2 hours before slicing.

COMMERCIAL BLEND RECIPE

Nutritional Information (per 100g)

Yield: 1 boule

For the preferment
- 50 grams active gluten-free sourdough starter
- 100 grams King Arthur measure for measure flour
- 100 grams warm water (75-83°F / 24-28°C)

For the dough
- 310 grams water
- 430 grams King Arthur measure for measure flour
- 12 grams salt

Calories	180
Carbohydrates	36g
Protein	3g
Fat	1g
Fiber	3g

Prepare the preferment

1. In a bowl, mix 50g of active gluten-free sourdough starter, 100g measure for measure flour, and 100g warm water. Gradually add the water to achieve a thick paste-like consistency.

2. Cover the bowl loosely and let the preferment sit at room temperature for 6-10 hours, or until it reaches its peak.

Prepare the dough

3. When the preferment is ready, whisk together the measure-for-measure flour and salt in a large bowl or the bowl of a stand mixer. Make sure the ingredients are thoroughly combined to ensure even distribution.

4. Add the preferment to the dry ingredients. If using a stand mixer with a dough hook or mixing by hand with a large spoon or spatula, start combining the ingredients until a dough begins to form. Knead the dough until it is smooth and all ingredients are fully incorporated.

5. Transfer the dough to a lightly floured surface and flatten it. Fold the sides of the dough over itself, flip it over, and shape it into a ball or oval depending on your proofing basket. Place the dough upside down in the banneton or in a bowl lined with a kitchen towel if you're not using a banneton. Cover the dough with a tea towel and let it proof for 3-5 hours, or until it is well-risen.

Bake

6. About 1 hour before baking preheat the oven to 450°F (235°C), with the Dutch oven, baking stone, or oven tray inside. If you're not using a Dutch oven, place a shallow metal pan at the bottom of the oven.

7. Gently invert the dough from the proofing basket onto a sheet of parchment paper and score the top. Then, using the edges of the parchment paper, carefully transfer the dough into the preheated vessel (Dutch oven, baking stone, or oven tray) and bake. If you're not using a Dutch oven, pour a cup of boiling water into the shallow pan at the bottom of the oven.

8. After about 25 minutes, remove the water pan or the lid of the Dutch oven, and continue baking for another 40-45 minutes. Once the bread is fully baked, take it out of the oven and let it cool for at least 2 hours before slicing.

CLASSIC BREADS

From the soft texture of a white sandwich loaf to the rustic charm of a country-style boule, this selection of recipes offers a variety of breads, each with its own unique aromas and flavors. While the taste profiles differ from one recipe to another, they remain well balanced and carefully crafted to complement a wide range of dishes.

These classic breads are ideal for everyday use, providing the perfect foundation for breakfast toast, a hearty sandwich, or to accompany a warm meal at dinner.

SANDWICH BREAD

Nutritional Information (per 100g)

Calories	200
Carbohydrates	40g
Protein	3g
Fat	4g
Fiber	5g

Yield: 1 loaf

For the preferment
- 50 grams active gluten-free sourdough starter
- 100 grams millet flour
- 100 grams warm water (75-83°F / 24-28°C)

For the dough
- 30 grams whole psyllium husk
- 420 grams water
- 100 grams millet flour
- 100 grams brown rice flour
- 65 grams tapioca starch
- 65 grams potato starch
- 20 grams oil
- 12 grams salt

Prepare the preferment

1. In a bowl, mix 50g of active gluten-free sourdough starter, 100g millet flour, and 100g warm water. Gradually add the water until you achieve a thick, paste-like consistency.
2. Cover the bowl loosely and let the preferment sit at room temperature for 6-10 hours, or until it reaches its peak.

Prepare the dough

3. When the preferment is ready, prepare the psyllium gel. In a medium bowl, vigorously whisk the psyllium husk with water for 30-60 seconds until fully incorporated. Let the mixture sit for about 5-10 minutes to fully hydrate and develop a gel-like texture.
4. In a large bowl or stand mixer, whisk together the flours, starches and salt. Ensure these ingredients are thoroughly mixed for even distribution.
5. Add the preferment to the psyllium gel. Mix thoroughly by hand, with a wooden spoon, or using an electric mixer until the mixture is smooth and well combined.
6. Add the psyllium-preferment gel mixture to the dry ingredients and then add the oil. If using a stand mixer with a dough hook or mixing by hand with a large spoon or spatula, start combining the ingredients until a dough begins to form. Knead the dough until it is smooth and all ingredients are fully incorporated.
7. Lightly grease the inside of a 2lb loaf pan with olive oil, or alternatively, line it with parchment paper.
8. Place the dough onto a lightly oiled surface, and gently press and stretch it into a rectangular shape that's just slightly smaller than the length of your loaf pan. Roll the dough from one of the shorter sides to form a log. Carefully transfer the dough into the loaf pan with the seam facing down,

cover it with a damp kitchen towel and let it proof for 3-5 hours, or until it is well-risen.

Bake

9. About 1 hour before baking preheat the oven to 425°F (220°C), placing a shallow metal pan at the bottom of the oven.
10. Gently brush the top of the bread with olive oil, then place it in the oven. Add a cup of boiling water to the metal pan and bake.
11. After about 25 minutes, remove the water pan and continue baking for another 35 minutes. Carefully take the bread out of the loaf pan and place it directly on the oven rack to bake for an additional 30 minutes. Be sure to check that the bread doesn't darken too quickly. If it does, simply cover it with a sheet of aluminum foil and continue baking.
12. Once the bread is fully baked, remove it from the oven and let it cool for at least 2 hours before slicing.

RUSTIC BOULE (LECTIN-FREE)

Yield: 1 boule

For the preferment
- 50 grams active gluten-free sourdough starter
- 100 grams sorghum flour
- 100 grams warm water (75-83°F / 24-28°C)

For the dough
- 20 grams whole psyllium husk
- 10 grams sugar or honey
- 10 grams olive oil
- 410 grams water
- 50 grams sorghum flour
- 80 grams teff flour
- 80 grams millet flour
- 70 grams tapioca flour
- 10 grams salt

Calories	180
Carbohydrates	37g
Protein	3g
Fat	3g
Fiber	4g

Prepare the preferment

1. In a bowl, mix 50g of active gluten-free sourdough starter, 100g sorghum flour, and 100g warm water. Gradually add the water to achieve a thick paste-like consistency.

2. Cover the bowl loosely and let the preferment sit at room temperature for 6-10 hours, or until it reaches its peak.

Prepare the dough

3. When the preferment is ready, prepare the psyllium gel. In a medium bowl, vigorously whisk the psyllium husk with water for 30-60 seconds until fully incorporated. Let the mixture sit for about 5-10 minutes to fully hydrate and develop a gel-like texture.

4. In a large bowl or stand mixer, whisk together the flours and salt. Ensure these ingredients are thoroughly mixed for even distribution.

5. Add the preferment and the sugar or honey to the psyllium gel. Mix thoroughly by hand, with a wooden spoon, or using an electric mixer until the mixture is smooth and well combined.

6. Add the psyllium-preferment gel mixture to the dry ingredients and then add the oil. If using a stand mixer with a dough hook or mixing by hand with a large spoon or spatula, start combining the ingredients until a dough begins to form. Knead the dough until it is smooth and all ingredients are fully incorporated. Cover the bowl with plastic wrap or a damp kitchen towel and let it ferment for about 1 hour.

7. Transfer the dough to a lightly floured surface and flatten it. Fold the sides of the dough over itself, flip it over, and shape it into a ball or oval depending on your proofing basket. Place the dough upside down in the banneton or in a bowl lined with a kitchen towel if you're not using a banneton. Cover the dough with a tea towel and let it proof for 2-4 hours, or until it is well-risen.

Bake

8. About 1 hour before baking preheat the oven to 450°F (235°C), with the Dutch oven, baking stone, or oven tray inside. If you're not using a Dutch oven, place a shallow metal pan at the bottom of the oven.

9. Gently invert the dough from the proofing basket onto a sheet of parchment paper and score the top. Then, using the edges of the parchment paper, carefully transfer the dough into the preheated vessel (Dutch oven, baking stone, or oven tray) and bake. If you're not using a Dutch oven, pour a cup of boiling water into the shallow pan at the bottom of the oven.

10. After about 25 minutes, remove the water pan or the lid of the Dutch oven, and continue baking for another 40-45 minutes. Once the bread is fully baked, take it out of the oven and let it cool for at least 2 hours before slicing.

RICE & SORGHUM BOULE

Yield: 1 boule

For the preferment
- 50 grams active gluten-free sourdough starter
- 100 grams brown rice flour
- 100 grams warm water (75-83°F / 24-28°C)

For the dough
- 20 grams whole psyllium husk
- 22 grams honey
- 15 grams olive oil
- 350 grams water
- 90 grams brown rice flour
- 100 grams sorghum flour
- 70 grams tapioca flour
- 70 grams potato starch
- 12 grams salt

Nutritional Information (per 100g)	
Calories	190
Carbohydrates	40g
Protein	3g
Fat	3g
Fiber	4g

Prepare the preferment

1. In a bowl, mix 50g of active gluten-free sourdough starter, 100g brown rice flour, and 100g warm water. Gradually add the water to achieve a thick paste-like consistency.

2. Cover the bowl loosely and let the preferment sit at room temperature for 6-10 hours, or until it reaches its peak.

Prepare the dough

3. When the preferment is ready, prepare the psyllium gel. In a medium bowl, vigorously whisk the psyllium husk with water for 30-60 seconds until fully incorporated. Let the mixture sit for about 5-10 minutes to fully hydrate and develop a gel-like texture.

4. In a large bowl or stand mixer, whisk together the flours, starches and salt. Ensure these ingredients are thoroughly mixed for even distribution.

5. Add the preferment and the honey to the psyllium gel. Mix thoroughly by hand, with a wooden spoon, or using an electric mixer until the mixture is smooth and well combined.

6. Add the psyllium-preferment gel mixture to the dry ingredients and then add the oil. If using a stand mixer with a dough hook or mixing by hand with a large spoon or spatula, start combining the ingredients until a dough begins to form. Knead the dough until it is smooth and all ingredients are fully incorporated.

7. Transfer the dough to a lightly floured surface and flatten it. Fold the sides of the dough over itself, flip it over, and shape it into a ball or oval depending on your proofing basket. Place the dough upside down in the banneton or in a bowl lined with a kitchen towel if you're not using a banneton. Cover the dough with a tea towel and let it proof for 3-5 hours, or until it is well-risen.

Bake

8. About 1 hour before baking preheat the oven to 425°F (220°C), with the Dutch oven, baking stone, or oven tray inside. If you're not using a Dutch oven, place a shallow metal pan at the bottom of the oven.

9. Gently invert the dough from the proofing basket onto a sheet of parchment paper and score the top. Then, using the edges of the parchment paper, carefully transfer the dough into the preheated vessel (Dutch oven, baking stone, or oven tray) and bake. If you're not using a Dutch oven, pour a cup of boiling water into the shallow pan at the bottom of the oven.

10. After about 25 minutes, remove the water pan or the lid of the Dutch oven, and continue baking for another 40-45 minutes. Once the bread is fully baked, take it out of the oven and let it cool for at least 2 hours before slicing.

ARTISAN BREAD

Yield: 1 boule

For the preferment
- 50 grams active gluten-free sourdough starter
- 100 grams millet flour
- 100 grams warm water (75-83°F / 24-28°C)

For the dough
- 25 grams whole psyllium husk
- 10 grams olive oil
- 320 grams water
- 70 grams buckwheat flour
- 100 grams millet flour
- 60 grams tapioca flour
- 40 grams potato starch
- 10 grams salt

Calories	185
Carbohydrates	38g
Protein	3g
Fat	2g
Fiber	4g

Prepare the preferment

1. In a bowl, mix 50g of active gluten-free sourdough starter, 100g millet flour, and 100g warm water. Gradually add the water to achieve a thick paste-like consistency.
2. Cover the bowl loosely and let the preferment sit at room temperature for 6-10 hours, or until it reaches its peak.

Prepare the dough

3. When the preferment is ready, prepare the psyllium gel. In a medium bowl, vigorously whisk the psyllium husk with water for 30-60 seconds until fully incorporated. Let the mixture sit for about 5-10 minutes to fully hydrate and develop a gel-like texture.
4. In a large bowl or stand mixer, whisk together the flours, starches and salt. Ensure these ingredients are thoroughly mixed for even distribution.
5. Add the preferment to the psyllium gel. Mix thoroughly by hand, with a wooden spoon, or using an electric mixer until the mixture is smooth and well combined.
6. Add the psyllium-preferment gel mixture to the dry ingredients and then add the oil. If using a stand mixer with a dough hook or mixing by hand with a large spoon or spatula, start combining the ingredients until a dough begins to form. Knead the dough until it is smooth and all ingredients are fully incorporated.

7. Transfer the dough to a lightly floured surface and flatten it. Fold the sides of the dough over itself, flip it over, and shape it into a ball or oval depending on your proofing basket. Place the dough upside down in the banneton or in a bowl lined with a kitchen towel if you're not using a banneton. Cover the dough with a tea towel and let it proof for 3-5 hours, or until it is well-risen.

Bake

8. About 1 hour before baking preheat the oven to 450°F (230°C), with the Dutch oven, baking stone, or oven tray inside. If you're not using a Dutch oven, place a shallow metal pan at the bottom of the oven.
9. Gently invert the dough from the proofing basket onto a sheet of parchment paper and score the top. Then, using the edges of the parchment paper, carefully transfer the dough into the preheated vessel (Dutch oven, baking stone, or oven tray) and bake. If you're not using a Dutch oven, pour a cup of boiling water into the shallow pan at the bottom of the oven.
10. After about 25 minutes, remove the water pan or the lid of the Dutch oven, and continue baking for another 45-50 minutes. Once the bread is fully baked, take it out of the oven and let it cool for at least 2 hours before slicing.

ROLLS BUNS & MORE

From soft and fluffy rolls to perfectly shaped buns, these recipes provide the ideal base for anything from everyday meals to special occasions. Whether you're looking for the perfect burger bun, a classic roll for sandwiches, or something a bit more unique, these options have you covered.

Each recipe is designed to create light and airy textures while still holding up to a range of fillings and flavors. These breads are not only great on their own, but they also elevate the dishes they accompany. Ideal for parties, picnics, or family dinners, these rolls and buns will quickly become staples in your kitchen.

MIXED SEEDS ROLLS

Yield: 10 rolls

For the preferment
- 50 grams active gluten-free sourdough starter
- 100 grams brown rice flour
- 100 grams warm water (75-83°F / 24-28°C)

For the dough
- 25 grams whole psyllium husk
- 330 grams water
- 120 grams sorghum flour
- 50 grams corn flour
- 60 grams potato starch
- 25 grams sunflower seeds
- 25 grams pumpkin seeds
- 10 grams salt

Nutritional Information (per roll)

Calories	150
Carbohydrates	30g
Protein	3g
Fat	2g
Fiber	4g

Prepare the preferment

1. In a bowl, mix 50g of active gluten-free sourdough starter, 100g brown rice flour, and 100g warm water. Gradually add the water to achieve a thick paste-like consistency.
2. Cover the bowl loosely and let the preferment sit at room temperature for 6-10 hours, or until it reaches its peak.

Prepare the dough

3. When the preferment is ready, prepare the psyllium gel. In a medium bowl, vigorously whisk the psyllium husk with water for 30-60 seconds until fully incorporated. Let the mixture sit for about 5-10 minutes to fully hydrate and develop a gel-like texture.
4. In a large bowl or stand mixer, whisk together the flours, potato starch, seeds and salt. Ensure these ingredients are thoroughly mixed for even distribution.
5. Add the preferment to the psyllium gel. Mix thoroughly by hand, with a wooden spoon, or using an electric mixer until the mixture is smooth and well combined.
6. Add the psyllium-preferment gel mixture to the dry ingredients. If using a stand mixer with a dough hook or mixing by hand with a large spoon or spatula, start combining the ingredients until a dough begins to form. Knead the dough until it is smooth and all ingredients are fully incorporated.

7. Transfer the dough to a lightly floured surface and divide in 10 equal pieces (about 90 grams each).
8. Shape each piece into a ball and place them seam-side down on an oven tray lined with parchment paper, leaving about 3 inches (8 cm) between each ball. Cover the tray with a damp kitchen towel or plastic wrap and let the dough proof for 3-5 hours, or until well risen.

Bake

9. About 1 hour before baking place a shallow metal pan on the bottom of the oven and preheat to 450°F (230°C).
10. Score the tops of the rolls, then place them on the middle rack. Carefully pour a cup of boiling water into the pan at the bottom of the oven.
11. After about 15 minutes, remove the water pan, and continue baking for another 15-20 minutes. Once the rolls are fully baked, remove them from the oven and let them cool for at least 2 hours.

SOFT ROLLS

Yield: 8 rolls

For the preferment
- 50 grams active gluten-free sourdough starter
- 100 grams brown rice flour
- 100 grams warm water (75-83°F / 24-28°C)

For the dough
- 25 grams whole psyllium husk
- 350 grams water
- 20 grams honey
- 20 grams olive oil
- 70 grams quinoa flour
- 100 grams brown rice flour
- 20 grams almond flour
- 70 grams tapioca flour
- 70 grams potato starch
- 12 grams salt

Calories	190
Carbohydrates	35g
Protein	3g
Fat	5g
Fiber	4g

Prepare the preferment

1. In a bowl, mix 50g of active gluten-free sourdough starter, 100g brown rice flour, and 100g warm water. Gradually add the water to achieve a thick paste-like consistency.
2. Cover the bowl loosely and let the preferment sit at room temperature for 6-10 hours, or until it reaches its peak.

Prepare the dough

3. When the preferment is ready, prepare the psyllium gel. In a medium bowl, vigorously whisk the psyllium husk with water for 30-60 seconds until fully incorporated. Let the mixture sit for about 5-10 minutes to fully hydrate and develop a gel-like texture.
4. In a large bowl or stand mixer, whisk together the flours, starches and salt. Ensure these ingredients are thoroughly mixed for even distribution.
5. Add the preferment and the honey to the psyllium gel. Mix thoroughly by hand, with a wooden spoon, or using an electric mixer until the mixture is smooth and well combined.
6. Add the psyllium-preferment gel mixture to the dry ingredients and then add the oil. If using a stand mixer with a dough hook or mixing by hand with a large spoon or spatula, start combining the ingredients until a dough begins to form. Knead the dough until it is smooth and all ingredients are fully incorporated.

7. Transfer the dough to a lightly floured surface and divide in 8 equal pieces (about 125 grams each).
8. Shape each piece into a ball and place them seam-side down on an oven tray lined with parchment paper, leaving about 4 inches (10 cm) between each ball. Cover the tray with a damp kitchen towel or plastic wrap and let the dough proof for 3-5 hours, or until well risen.

Bake

9. About 1 hour before baking place a shallow metal pan on the bottom of the oven and preheat to 425°F (220°C).
10. Brush each roll with olive oil and score the tops, then place them on the middle rack. Carefully pour a cup of boiling water into the pan at the bottom of the oven.
11. After about 15 minutes, remove the water pan and continue baking for another 25-30 minutes. Once the rolls are fully baked, remove them from the oven and let them cool for at least 2 hours.

ITALIAN CIABATTA

Yield: 4 ciabatta loaves

For the preferment
- 50 grams active gluten-free sourdough starter
- 100 grams millet flour
- 100 grams warm water (75-83°F / 24-28°C)

For the dough
- 20 grams whole psyllium husk
- 20 grams olive oil
- 330 grams water
- 40 grams millet
- 80 grams sorghum flour
- 20 grams almond flour
- 60 grams potato starch
- 60 tapioca flour
- 8 grams salt

Calories	220
Carbohydrates	40g
Protein	4g
Fat	5g
Fiber	4g

Prepare the preferment

1. In a bowl, mix 50g of active gluten-free sourdough starter, 100g millet flour, and 100g warm water. Gradually add the water to achieve a thick paste-like consistency.
2. Cover the bowl loosely and let the preferment sit at room temperature for 6-10 hours, or until it reaches its peak.

Prepare the dough

3. When the preferment is ready, prepare the psyllium gel. In a medium bowl, vigorously whisk the psyllium husk with water for 30-60 seconds until fully incorporated. Let the mixture sit for about 5-10 minutes to fully hydrate and develop a gel-like texture.
4. In a large bowl or stand mixer, whisk together the flours, starches and salt. Ensure these ingredients are thoroughly mixed for even distribution.
5. Add the preferment to the psyllium gel. Mix thoroughly by hand, with a wooden spoon, or using an electric mixer until the mixture is smooth and well combined.
6. Add the psyllium-preferment gel mixture to the dry ingredients and then add the oil. If using a stand mixer with a dough hook or mixing by hand with a large spoon or spatula, start combining the ingredients until a dough begins to form. Knead the dough until it is smooth and all ingredients are fully incorporated.
7. Transfer the dough to a generously floured surface and gently press and stretch it into a 5 x 16 inch (15 x 40 cm) rectangle. Using a knife or bench scraper, divide the rectangle into 4

equal pieces, each about 5 x 4 inches (15 x 10 cm). Place the pieces on a baking sheet lined with parchment paper, with the floured sides facing up, ensuring they are about 4 inches (10 cm) apart. Cover with a damp kitchen towel or plastic wrap and let it proof for 3-5 hours, or until it has risen well.

Bake

8. About 1 hour before baking place a shallow metal pan on the bottom of the oven and preheat to 425°F (220°C).
9. Place the ciabatta loaves on the middle rack of the oven. Carefully pour a cup of boiling water into the pan at the bottom of the oven.
10. After about 15 minutes, remove the water pan, and continue baking for another 20-25 minutes. Once the ciabatta loaves are fully baked, remove them from the oven and let them cool for at least 2 hours.

CLASSIC ROLLS

Yield: 8 rolls

For the preferment
- 50 grams active gluten-free sourdough starter
- 100 grams brown rice flour
- 100 grams warm water (75-83°F / 24-28°C)

For the dough
- 25 grams whole psyllium husk
- 300 grams water
- 80 grams millet flour
- 40 grams brown rice flour
- 65 grams tapioca flour
- 65 grams potato starch
- 9 grams salt

Calories	150
Carbohydrates	31g
Protein	3g
Fat	1g
Fiber	4g

Prepare the preferment

1. In a bowl, mix 50g of active gluten-free sourdough starter, 100g brown rice flour, and 100g warm water. Gradually add the water to achieve a thick paste-like consistency.
2. Cover the bowl loosely and let the preferment sit at room temperature for 6-10 hours, or until it reaches its peak.

Prepare the dough

3. When the preferment is ready, prepare the psyllium gel. In a medium bowl, vigorously whisk the psyllium husk with water for 30-60 seconds until fully incorporated. Let the mixture sit for about 5-10 minutes to fully hydrate and develop a gel-like texture.
4. In a large bowl or stand mixer, whisk together the flours, starches and salt. Ensure these ingredients are thoroughly mixed for even distribution.

5. Add the preferment to the psyllium gel. Mix thoroughly by hand, with a wooden spoon, or using an electric mixer until the mixture is smooth and well combined.
6. Add the psyllium-preferment gel mixture to the dry ingredients. If using a stand mixer with a dough hook or mixing by hand with a large spoon or spatula, start combining the ingredients until a dough begins to form. Knead the dough until it is smooth and all ingredients are fully incorporated.
7. Transfer the dough to a lightly floured surface and divide in 8 equal pieces (about 100-105 grams each).
8. Shape each piece into a ball and place them seam-side down on an oven tray lined with parchment paper, leaving about 3 inches (8 cm) between each ball. Cover the tray with a damp kitchen towel or plastic wrap and let the dough proof for 3-5 hours, or until well risen.

Bake

9. About 1 hour before baking place a shallow metal pan on the bottom of the oven and preheat to 450°F (230°C).
10. Score the tops of the rolls, then place them on the middle rack. Carefully pour a cup of boiling water into the pan at the bottom of the oven.
11. After about 15 minutes, remove the water pan, reduce the oven temperature to 415°F (210°C) and continue baking for another 25-30 minutes. Once the rolls are fully baked, remove them from the oven and let them cool for at least 2 hours.

BURGER BUNS

Yield: 6 buns

For the preferment
- 50 grams active gluten-free sourdough starter
- 100 grams millet flour
- 100 grams warm water (75-83°F / 24-28°C)

For the dough
- 23 grams whole psyllium husk
- 230 grams water
- 20 grams honey
- 30 grams unsalted butter

- 60 grams millet flour
- 20 grams almond flour
- 70 grams tapioca flour
- 70 grams potato starch
- 10 grams salt

For the topping
- 1 egg yolk
- 1 TBSP water
- sesame seeds
- melted unsalted butter

Calories	260
Carbohydrates	42g
Protein	4g
Fat	7g
Fiber	5g

Prepare the preferment

1. In a bowl, mix 50g of active gluten-free sourdough starter, 100g millet flour, and 100g warm water. Gradually add the water to achieve a thick paste-like consistency.
2. Cover the bowl loosely and let the preferment sit at room temperature for 6-10 hours, or until it reaches its peak.

Prepare the dough

3. When the preferment is ready, prepare the psyllium gel. In a medium bowl, vigorously whisk the psyllium husk with water for 30-60 seconds until fully incorporated. Let the mixture sit for about 5-10 minutes to fully hydrate and develop a gel-like texture.
4. In a large bowl or stand mixer, whisk together the flours, starches and salt. Ensure these ingredients are thoroughly mixed for even distribution.
5. Add the preferment and the honey to the psyllium gel. Mix thoroughly by hand, with a wooden spoon, or using an electric mixer until the mixture is smooth and well combined.
6. Add the psyllium-preferment gel mixture to the dry ingredients and then add the softened butter. If using a stand mixer with a dough hook or mixing by hand with a large spoon or spatula, start combining the ingredients until a dough begins to form. Knead the dough until it is smooth and all ingredients are fully incorporated. The resulting dough will be very soft and sticky due to the high hydration and the presence of butter.
7. Transfer the dough to a lightly oiled surface and divide in 6 equal pieces (about 130 grams each).
8. Shape each piece into a ball, then gently flat-

ten each ball slightly to give it the classic burger bun shape. Place them seam-side down on an oven tray lined with parchment paper, leaving about 4 inches (10 cm) between each one. Cover the tray with a damp kitchen towel or plastic wrap and let the dough proof for 3-5 hours, or until well risen.

Bake

9. About 1 hour before baking place a shallow metal pan on the bottom of the oven and preheat to 400°F (200°C).
10. Whisk the egg yolk with a tablespoon of water, then brush the mixture over each bun. Sprinkle the buns with sesame seeds and place them on the middle rack. Carefully pour a cup of boiling water into the pan at the bottom of the oven.
11. After about 10 minutes, remove the water pan and continue baking for another 25-30 minutes. Once the rolls are fully baked, take them out of the oven, brush them with melted butter, and allow them to cool for at least 2 hours.

SPECIAL BREADS

These recipes offer a chance to play with bold flavor combinations and inventive textures, allowing you to create something truly distinctive. Whether you're looking for a hearty option to pair with a special meal or simply want to surprise your family with something new, these breads bring a touch of creativity to the table.

Each bread offers a fresh take on familiar flavors, turning the everyday into something memorable. Whether it's the rich depth of a savory loaf or the unexpected sweetness of a special treat, these breads promise to awaken your senses and add a new layer of excitement to your baking repertoire.

RYE LIKE BREAD

Yield: 1 loaf

For the preferment
- 50 grams active gluten-free sourdough starter
- 100 grams teff flour
- 100 grams warm water (75-83°F / 24-28°C)

For the dough
- 25 grams whole psyllium husk
- 40 grams maple syrup
- 400 grams water
- 130 grams buckwheat flour
- 100 grams sorghum flour
- 90 grams quinoa flour
- 12 grams flax seeds
- 40 grams pumpkin seeds
- 10 grams salt

Nutritional Information (per 100g)

Calories	230
Carbohydrates	40g
Protein	5g
Fat	5g
Fiber	6g

Prepare the preferment

1. In a bowl, mix 50g of active gluten-free sourdough starter, 100g teff flour, and 100g warm water. Gradually add the water to achieve a thick paste-like consistency.
2. Cover the bowl loosely and let the preferment sit at room temperature for 6-10 hours, or until it reaches its peak.

Prepare the dough

3. When the preferment is ready, prepare the psyllium gel. In a medium bowl, vigorously whisk the psyllium husk with water for 30-60 seconds until fully incorporated. Let the mixture sit for about 5-10 minutes to fully hydrate and develop a gel-like texture.
4. In a large bowl or stand mixer, whisk together the flours and salt. Ensure these ingredients are thoroughly mixed for even distribution.
5. Add the preferment and the maple syrup to the psyllium gel. Mix thoroughly by hand, with a wooden spoon, or using an electric mixer until the mixture is smooth and well combined.
6. Add the psyllium-preferment gel mixture to the dry ingredients and then add the seeds. If using a stand mixer with a dough hook or mixing by hand with a large spoon or spatula, start combining the ingredients until a dough begins to form. Knead the dough until it is smooth and all ingredients are fully incorporated.

7. Lightly grease the inside of a 2lb loaf pan with olive oil, or alternatively, line it with parchment paper.
8. Place the dough onto a lightly oiled surface, and gently press and stretch it into a rectangular shape that's just slightly smaller than the length of your loaf pan. Roll the dough from one of the shorter sides to form a log. Carefully transfer the dough into the loaf pan with the seam facing down, cover it with a damp kitchen towel and let it proof for 3-5 hours, or until it is well-risen.

Bake

9. About 1 hour before baking preheat the oven to 425°F (220°C), placing a shallow metal pan at the bottom of the oven.
10. Gently brush the top of the bread with olive oil, then place it in the oven. Add a cup of boiling water to the metal pan and bake.
11. After about 25 minutes, remove the water pan and continue baking for another 25 minutes. Carefully take the bread out of the loaf pan and place it directly on the oven rack to bake for an additional 10-20 minutes. Be sure to check that the bread doesn't darken too quickly. If it does, simply cover it with a sheet of aluminum foil and continue baking. Once the bread is fully baked, remove it from the oven and let it cool for at least 2 hours before slicing.

MULTIGRAIN BREAD

Yield: 1 boule

For the preferment
- 50 grams active gluten-free sourdough starter
- 100 grams millet flour
- 100 grams warm water (75-83°F / 24-28°C)

For the dough
- 25 grams whole psyllium husk
- 300 grams water
- 20 grams honey
- 20 grams olive oil
- 50 grams millet flour
- 50 sorghum flour
- 40 quinoa flour
- 50 grams tapioca flour
- 50 grams potato starch
- 25 grams sunflower seeds
- 25 grams pumpkin seeds
- 10 grams salt

Calories	220
Carbohydrates	37g
Protein	4g
Fat	6g
Fiber	5g

Prepare the preferment

1. In a bowl, mix 50g of active gluten-free sourdough starter, 100g millet flour, and 100g warm water. Gradually add the water to achieve a thick paste-like consistency.
2. Cover the bowl loosely and let the preferment sit at room temperature for 6-10 hours, or until it reaches its peak.

Prepare the dough

3. When the preferment is ready, prepare the psyllium gel. In a medium bowl, vigorously whisk the psyllium husk with water for 30-60 seconds until fully incorporated. Let the mixture sit for about 5-10 minutes to fully hydrate and develop a gel-like texture.
4. In a large bowl or stand mixer, whisk together flours, starches, seeds and salt. Ensure these ingredients are thoroughly mixed for even distribution.
5. Add the preferment and the honey to the psyllium gel. Mix thoroughly by hand, with a wooden spoon, or using an electric mixer until the mixture is smooth and well combined.
6. Add the psyllium-preferment gel mixture to the dry ingredients and then add the olive oil. If using a stand mixer with a dough hook or mixing by hand with a large spoon or spatula, start combining the ingredients until a dough begins to form. Knead the dough until it is smooth and all ingredients are fully incorporated.
7. Transfer the dough to a lightly floured surface and flatten it. Fold the sides of the dough over itself, flip it over, and shape it into a ball or oval depending on your proofing basket. Place the dough upside down in the banneton or in a bowl lined with a kitchen towel if you're not using a banneton. Cover the dough with a tea

towel and let it proof for 3-5 hours, or until it is well-risen.

Bake

8. About 1 hour before baking preheat the oven to 450°F (235°C), with the Dutch oven, baking stone, or oven tray inside. If you're not using a Dutch oven, place a shallow metal pan at the bottom of the oven.
9. Gently invert the dough from the proofing basket onto a sheet of parchment paper and score the top. Then, using the edges of the parchment paper, carefully transfer the dough into the preheated vessel (Dutch oven, baking stone, or oven tray) and bake. If you're not using a Dutch oven, pour a cup of boiling water into the shallow pan at the bottom of the oven.
10. After about 25 minutes, remove the water pan or the lid of the Dutch oven, and continue baking for another 45-50 minutes. Once the bread is fully baked, take it out of the oven and let it cool for at least 2 hours before slicing.

CHOCOLATE BREAD

Yield: 1 boule

For the preferment
- 50 grams active gluten-free sourdough starter
- 100 grams brown rice flour
- 100 grams warm water (75-83°F / 24-28°C)

For the dough
- 20 grams whole psyllium husk
- 20 grams maple syrup
- 15 grams olive oil
- 350 grams water
- 100 grams brown rice flour
- 90 grams sorghum flour
- 70 grams tapioca flour
- 70 grams potato starch
- 30 grams cacao powder
- 15 grams sugar
- 70 grams chocolate chips
- 70 grams hazelnuts
- 12 grams salt

Calories	280
Carbohydrates	40g
Protein	5g
Fat	10g
Fiber	6g

Prepare the preferment

1. In a bowl, mix 50g of active gluten-free sourdough starter, 100g brown rice flour, and 100g warm water. Gradually add the water to achieve a thick paste-like consistency.
2. Cover the bowl loosely and let the preferment sit at room temperature for 6-10 hours, or until it reaches its peak.

Prepare the dough

3. When the preferment is ready, prepare the psyllium gel. In a medium bowl, vigorously whisk the psyllium husk with water for 30-60 seconds until fully incorporated. Let the mixture sit for about 5-10 minutes to fully hydrate and develop a gel-like texture.
4. In a large bowl or stand mixer, whisk together the flours, sugar, cacao powder, starches and salt. Ensure these ingredients are thoroughly mixed for even distribution.
5. Add the preferment and the maple syrup to the psyllium gel. Mix thoroughly by hand, with a wooden spoon, or using an electric mixer until the mixture is smooth and well combined.

6. Add the psyllium-preferment gel mixture to the dry ingredients and then add the oil, chocolate chips and hazelnuts. If using a stand mixer with a dough hook or mixing by hand with a large spoon or spatula, start combining the ingredients until a dough begins to form. Knead the dough until it is smooth and all ingredients are fully incorporated.
7. Transfer the dough to a lightly floured surface and flatten it. Fold the sides of the dough over itself, flip it over, and shape it into a ball or oval depending on your proofing basket. Place the dough upside down in the banneton or in a bowl lined with a kitchen towel if you're not using a banneton. Cover the dough with a tea towel and let it proof for 3-5 hours, or until it is well-risen.

Bake

8. About 1 hour before baking preheat the oven to 425°F (220°C), with the Dutch oven, baking stone, or oven tray inside. If you're not using a Dutch oven, place a shallow metal pan at the bottom of the oven.
9. Gently invert the dough from the proofing basket onto a sheet of parchment paper and score the top. Then, using the edges of the parchment paper, carefully transfer the dough into the preheated vessel (Dutch oven, baking stone, or oven tray) and bake. If you're not using a Dutch oven, pour a cup of boiling water into the shallow pan at the bottom of the oven.
10. After about 25 minutes, remove the water pan or the lid of the Dutch oven, and continue baking for another 45-50 minutes. Once the bread is fully baked, take it out of the oven and let it cool for at least 2 hours before slicing.

CINNAMON BREAD

Calories	240
Carbohydrates	50g
Protein	3g
Fat	1g
Fiber	4g

Yield: 1 boule

For the preferment
- 50 grams active gluten-free sourdough starter
- 100 grams brown rice flour
- 100 grams warm water (75-83°F / 24-28°C)

For the dough
- 20 grams whole psyllium husk
- 20 grams honey
- 300 grams water
- 60 grams brown rice flour
- 60 grams sorghum flour
- 90 grams tapioca flour
- 90 grams potato starch
- 100 grams raisins
- 30 grams brown sugar
- 8 grams cinnamon powder
- 10 grams salt

Prepare the preferment

1. In a bowl, mix 50g of active gluten-free sourdough starter, 100g brown rice flour, and 100g warm water. Gradually add the water to achieve a thick paste-like consistency.
2. Cover the bowl loosely and let the preferment sit at room temperature for 6-10 hours, or until it reaches its peak.

Prepare the dough

3. When the preferment is ready, prepare the psyllium gel. In a medium bowl, vigorously whisk the psyllium husk with water for 30-60 seconds until fully incorporated. Let the mixture sit for about 5-10 minutes to fully hydrate and develop a gel-like texture.
4. In a large bowl or stand mixer, whisk together the flours, sugar, cinnamon powder, starches and salt. Ensure these ingredients are thoroughly mixed for even distribution.
5. Add the preferment and the honey to the psyllium gel. Mix thoroughly by hand, with a wooden spoon, or using an electric mixer until the mixture is smooth and well combined.
6. Add the psyllium-preferment gel mixture to the dry ingredients and then add raisins. If using a stand mixer with a dough hook or mixing by hand with a large spoon or spatula, start combining the ingredients until a dough begins to form. Knead the dough until it is smooth and all ingredients are fully incorporated.
7. Transfer the dough to a lightly floured surface and flatten it. Fold the sides of the dough over itself, flip it over, and shape it into a ball or oval depending on your proofing basket. Place the dough upside down in the banneton or in a bowl lined with a kitchen towel if you're not using a banneton. Cover the dough with a tea

towel and let it proof for 3-5 hours, or until it is well-risen.

Bake

8. About 1 hour before baking preheat the oven to 425°F (220°C), with the Dutch oven, baking stone, or oven tray inside. If you're not using a Dutch oven, place a shallow metal pan at the bottom of the oven.
9. Gently invert the dough from the proofing basket onto a sheet of parchment paper and score the top. Then, using the edges of the parchment paper, carefully transfer the dough into the preheated vessel (Dutch oven, baking stone, or oven tray) and bake. If you're not using a Dutch oven, pour a cup of boiling water into the shallow pan at the bottom of the oven.
10. After about 25 minutes, remove the water pan or the lid of the Dutch oven, and continue baking for another 40-45 minutes. Once the bread is fully baked, take it out of the oven and let it cool for at least 2 hours before slicing.

CHEDDAR AND JALAPEÑO BREAD

Nutritional Information (per 100g)

Yield: 1 boule

For the preferment
- 50 grams active gluten-free sourdough starter
- 100 grams brown rice flour
- 100 grams warm water (75-83°F / 24-28°C)

For the dough
- 25 grams whole psyllium husk
- 20 grams honey
- 250 grams water
- 80 grams sorghum flour
- 90 grams tapioca flour
- 90 grams potato starch
- 110 grams cheddar cheese
- 30 grams chopped jalapenos
- 8 grams baking powder
- 10 grams salt

Calories	240
Carbohydrates	38g
Protein	7g
Fat	6g
Fiber	5g

Prepare the preferment

1. In a bowl, mix 50g of active gluten-free sourdough starter, 100g brown rice flour, and 100g warm water. Gradually add the water to achieve a thick paste-like consistency.

2. Cover the bowl loosely and let the preferment sit at room temperature for 6-10 hours, or until it reaches its peak.

Prepare the dough

3. When the preferment is ready, prepare the psyllium gel. In a medium bowl, vigorously whisk the psyllium husk with water for 30-60 seconds until fully incorporated. Let the mixture sit for about 5-10 minutes to fully hydrate and develop a gel-like texture.

4. In a large bowl or stand mixer, whisk together the flours, baking powder, starches and salt. Ensure these ingredients are thoroughly mixed for even distribution.

5. Add the preferment and the honey to the psyllium gel. Mix thoroughly by hand, with a wooden spoon, or using an electric mixer until the mixture is smooth and well combined.

6. Shred the cheddar cheese and chop the jalapenos.

7. Add the psyllium-preferment gel mixture to the dry ingredients and then add the shredded cheddar and chopped jalapenos. If using a stand mixer with a dough hook or mixing by hand with a large spoon or spatula, start combining the ingredients until a dough begins to form. Knead the dough until it is smooth and all ingredients are fully incorporated.

8. Transfer the dough to a lightly floured surface and flatten it. Fold the sides of the dough over itself, flip it over, and shape it into a ball or oval depending on your proofing basket. Place the dough upside down in the banneton or in a bowl lined with a kitchen towel if you're not using a banneton. Cover the dough with a tea towel and let it proof for 3-5 hours, or until it is well-risen.

Bake

9. About 1 hour before baking preheat the oven to 425°F (220°C), with the Dutch oven, baking stone, or oven tray inside. If you're not using a Dutch oven, place a shallow metal pan at the bottom of the oven.

10. Gently invert the dough from the proofing basket onto a sheet of parchment paper and score the top. Then, using the edges of the parchment paper, carefully transfer the dough into the preheated vessel (Dutch oven, baking stone, or oven tray) and bake. If you're not using a Dutch oven, pour a cup of boiling water into the shallow pan at the bottom of the oven.

11. After about 25 minutes, remove the water pan or the lid of the Dutch oven, and continue baking for another 45-50 minutes. Once the bread is fully baked, take it out of the oven and let it cool for at least 2 hours before slicing.

FLATBREAD

Nutritional Information (per flatbread)

Yield: 8 flatbreads

For the preferment
- 30 grams active gluten-free sourdough starter
- 60 grams brown rice flour
- 60 grams warm water (75-83°F / 24-28°C)

For the dough
- 20 grams whole psyllium husk
- 15 grams honey
- 10 grams olive oil
- 350 grams water
- 130 grams sorghum flour
- 80 grams brown rice flour
- 50 grams potato starch
- 8 grams salt

For topping
- Flaky salt
- Extra virgin olive oil
- Dry oregano or dry rosmary

Calories	160
Carbohydrates	32g
Protein	3g
Fat	3g
Fiber	4g

Prepare the preferment

1. In a bowl, mix 30g of active gluten-free sourdough starter, 60g brown rice flour, and 60g warm water. Gradually add the water to achieve a thick paste-like consistency.
2. Cover the bowl loosely and let the preferment sit at room temperature for 6-10 hours, or until it reaches its peak.

Prepare the dough

3. When the preferment is ready, prepare the psyllium gel. In a medium bowl, vigorously whisk the psyllium husk with water for 30-60 seconds until fully incorporated. Let the mixture sit for about 5-10 minutes to fully hydrate and develop a gel-like texture.
4. In a large bowl or stand mixer, whisk together the flours, starches and salt. Ensure these ingredients are thoroughly mixed for even distribution.
5. Add the preferment and the honey to the psyllium gel. Mix thoroughly by hand, with a wooden spoon, or using an electric mixer until the mixture is smooth and well combined.
6. Add the psyllium-preferment gel mixture to the dry ingredients and then add the oil. If using a stand mixer with a dough hook or mixing by hand with a large spoon or spatula, start combining the ingredients until a dough begins to form. Knead the dough until it is smooth and all ingredients are fully incorporated.
7. Transfer the dough to a lightly floured surface and flatten it. Fold the sides of the dough over itself, flip it over, and shape it into a ball or oval depending on your proofing basket. Place the dough upside down in the banneton or in a bowl lined with a kitchen towel if you're not using a banneton. Cover the dough with a tea towel and let it proof for 3-5 hours, or until it is well-risen.

Bake

8. About 40 minutes before baking, preheat the oven to 480°F (250°C). If using a baking steel or pizza stone, place it on the middle oven rack at

this time.

9. Turn the dough out onto a lightly floured surface and, using a bench scraper or knife, divide it into 8 equal pieces, each weighing about 100g. Lightly oil your hands to prevent sticking, then shape each piece into a ball. Use a rolling pin to press and stretch a ball into a thickness of about ¼ inch (6mm), then transfer it onto parchment paper, placing two flatbreads per sheet, and cover with a towel to prevent drying. Continue with the remaining pieces, keeping each covered as you work.
10. Brush a light layer of olive oil on the surface of each flatbread and sprinkle with flaky sea salt and dried oregano or rosemary. When ready to bake, take one sheet of parchment paper with two flatbreads and place it onto the baking tray. If using a baking steel or pizza stone, carefully transfer the flatbread along with the parchment paper directly onto the preheated baking steel or pizza stone. Bake for about 10-15 minutes, or until golden brown.
11. Remove from the oven and let the flatbreads cool for at least 1 hour. Repeat the baking process with the remaining flatbreads, baking two at a time until all are done.

BEYOND BREADS

Moving beyond the typical loaf, these recipes offer practical options for a range of needs, from snacks to meal accompaniments. The goal here is to explore how dough can be shaped and baked into various forms, providing more diversity in both texture and flavor.

With every bake, you'll unlock new textures and flavors, showing just how much potential your sourdough starter truly has. Whether you're looking for something with a soft crumb for a casual meal or a crisp bite for something more substantial, these options are designed to offer dependable results. They allow you to experiment with different types of baked goods while still maintaining simplicity and ease in your kitchen routine.

FOCACCIA

Yield: 1 focaccia

For the preferment
- 50 grams active gluten-free sourdough starter
- 100 grams millet flour
- 100 grams warm water (75-83°F / 24-28°C)

For the dough
- 23 grams whole psyllium husk
- 270 grams water

- 35 grams olive oil
- 100 grams sorghum flour
- 40 grams white rice flour
- 80 grams tapioca flour
- 40 grams potato starch
- 10 grams salt

For the topping
- Extra-virgin olive oil
- Flake salt

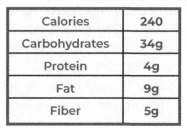

Nutritional Information (per 100g)

Calories	240
Carbohydrates	34g
Protein	4g
Fat	9g
Fiber	5g

Prepare the preferment

1. In a bowl, mix 50g of active gluten-free sourdough starter, 100g millet flour, and 100g warm water. Gradually add the water to achieve a thick paste-like consistency.
2. Cover the bowl loosely and let the preferment sit at room temperature for 6-10 hours, or until it reaches its peak.

Prepare the dough

3. When the preferment is ready, prepare the psyllium gel. In a medium bowl, vigorously whisk the psyllium husk with water for 30-60 seconds until fully incorporated. Let the mixture sit for about 5-10 minutes to fully hydrate and develop a gel-like texture.

4. In a large bowl or stand mixer, whisk together the flours, starches and salt. Ensure these ingredients are thoroughly mixed for even distribution.
5. Add the preferment to the psyllium gel. Mix thoroughly by hand, with a wooden spoon, or using an electric mixer until the mixture is smooth and well combined.
6. Add the psyllium-preferment gel mixture to the dry ingredients and then add the olive oil. If using a stand mixer with a dough hook or mixing by hand with a large spoon or spatula, start combining the ingredients until a dough begins to form. Knead the dough until it is smooth and all ingredients are fully incorporated.
7. Grease a 7×9" oven tray with olive oil and place the dough inside. Using your wet fingers, start at the center of the dough and gently press outward toward the edges, spreading the dough to fill the bottom of the tray. Cover with a damp kitchen towel or plastic wrap, and let the dough proof for 3-5 hours, or until well risen.

Bake

8. About 1 hour before baking, preheat the oven to 425°F (220°C).
9. Brush the focaccia generously with olive oil and use your fingers to create dimples in the dough. Season with flaky sea salt and place the tray in the lower part of the preheated oven.
10. Bake the focaccia for about 30-40 minutes, or until golden brown. If it begins to darken too quickly, cover it with a sheet of aluminum foil and continue baking for the remaining time. Let it cool for at least 2 hours before serving.

BAGELS

Yield: 8 bagels

For the preferment
- 50 grams active gluten-free sourdough starter
- 100 grams brown rice flour
- 100 grams warm water (75-83°F / 24-28°C)

For the dough
- 27 grams whole psyllium husk
- 230 grams water
- 20 grams honey
- 25 grams olive oil

- 70 grams millet flour
- 40 grams brown rice flour
- 65 grams tapioca flour
- 65 grams potato starch
- 10 grams salt

For the boiling
- 2 ½ tbsp baking soda
- 2 tbsp maple syrup

For the topping
- Olive oil
- Sesame and poppy seeds

Calories	220
Carbohydrates	40g
Protein	4g
Fat	5g
Fiber	5g

Prepare the preferment

1. In a bowl, mix 50g of active gluten-free sourdough starter, 100g brown rice flour, and 100g warm water. Gradually add the water to achieve a thick paste-like consistency.
2. Cover the bowl loosely and let the preferment sit at room temperature for 6-10 hours, or until it reaches its peak.

Prepare the dough

3. When the preferment is ready, prepare the psyllium gel. In a medium bowl, vigorously whisk the psyllium husk with water for 30-60 seconds until fully incorporated. Let the mixture sit for about 5-10 minutes to fully hydrate and develop a gel-like texture.
4. In a large bowl or stand mixer, whisk together the flours, starches and salt. Ensure these ingredients are thoroughly mixed for even distribution.
5. Add the preferment and the honey to the psyllium gel. Mix thoroughly by hand, with a wooden spoon, or using an electric mixer until the mixture is smooth and well combined.
6. Add the psyllium-preferment gel mixture to the dry ingredients and then add the olive oil. If using a stand mixer with a dough hook or mixing by hand with a large spoon or spatula, start combining the ingredients until a dough begins to form. Knead the dough until it is smooth and all ingredients are fully incorporated.
7. Transfer the dough to a lightly oiled surface and divide it into 8 equal pieces (about 100 grams each). Shape each piece into a ball, then use your lightly oiled index finger to poke a hole through the center of each ball. Gently expand the hole until it's about 1 inch (2,5cm) in diameter. Place the bagels on an oven tray

lined with parchment paper, leaving about 4 inches (10 cm) of space between them. Cover the tray with a damp kitchen towel or plastic wrap, and let the dough proof for 3-5 hours, or until well risen.

Bake

8. About 1 hour before baking, preheat the oven to 415°F (210°C). Fill a wide pot with about 3 quarts (3 liters) of water, then add the maple syrup and baking soda, and bring to a boil. Once boiling, cook 4-5 bagels at a time, ensuring they have enough space between them. Cook for about 1 minute per side. After boiling, place them on a kitchen towel to dry.
9. Place the bagels on an oven tray lined with parchment paper and brush them with olive oil. Then sprinkle poppy seeds and sesame seeds on top. Bake them on the middle rack of the oven for 30-35 minutes.
10. Once the bagels are fully baked, remove them from the oven and let them cool for at least 2 hours.

ENGLISH MUFFINS

Yield: 8 muffins

For the preferment
- 40 grams active gluten-free sourdough starter
- 80 grams brown rice flour
- 80 grams warm water (75-83°F / 24-28°C)

For the dough
- 20 grams whole psyllium husk
- 220 grams water
- 75 grams plant based milk or regular milk
- 20 grams honey
- 100 grams sorghum flour
- 50 grams white rice flour
- 50 grams tapioca flour
- 50 grams potato starch
- 10 grams baking powder
- 8 grams salt

For the topping
- cornmeal

Calories	180
Carbohydrates	35g
Protein	3g
Fat	3g
Fiber	4g

Prepare the preferment

1. In a bowl, mix 40g of active gluten-free sourdough starter, 80g brown rice flour, and 80g warm water. Gradually add the water to achieve a thick paste-like consistency.
2. Cover the bowl loosely and let the preferment sit at room temperature for 6-10 hours, or until it reaches its peak.

Prepare the dough

3. When the preferment is ready, prepare the psyllium gel. In a medium bowl, vigorously whisk the psyllium husk with water for 30-60 seconds until fully incorporated. Let the mixture sit for about 5-10 minutes to fully hydrate and develop a gel-like texture.
4. In a large bowl or stand mixer, whisk together the flours, starches, baking powder and salt. Ensure these ingredients are thoroughly mixed for even distribution.
5. Add the preferment and the honey to the psyllium gel. Mix thoroughly by hand, with a wooden spoon, or using an electric mixer until the mixture is smooth and well combined.
6. Add the psyllium-preferment gel mixture to the dry ingredients and then add the milk. If using a stand mixer with a dough hook or mixing by hand with a large spoon or spatula, start combining the ingredients until a dough begins to form. Knead the dough until it is smooth and all ingredients are fully incorporated. The resulting dough will be very soft and sticky due to the high hydration and the presence of butter.
7. Turn the dough out onto a lightly floured surface and shape it into a ball. Using a bench scraper or knife, divide the dough into 8 equal pieces, each weighing about 100g. Lightly oil your hands to prevent sticking, then shape each piece into a ball and gently press it into a disc flattening it to about 1 1/5 inches (4cm) thick. Pour some cornmeal onto a plate and dip both sides of each disc in the cornmeal to avoid sticking during cooking. Place the shaped muffins on an oven tray lined with parchment paper, cover them with a tea towel, and let them proof for 3-5 hours.

Bake

8. Preheat the oven to 350°F (175°C). Heat a large skillet over medium heat and add oil. Cook the muffins in the preheated skillet for about 4 minutes on each side, or until golden brown.
9. Transfer the muffins to the oven tray and bake for an additional 20 minutes in the oven. Let them cool for at least 2 hours before serving.

PIZZA CRUST

Yield: 5 pizzas

For the preferment
- 50 grams active gluten-free sourdough starter
- 100 grams sorghum flour
- 100 grams warm water (75-83°F / 24-28°C)

For the dough
- 35 grams whole psyllium husk
- 470 grams water
- 30 grams olive oil
- 180 grams sorghum flour
- 60 grams white rice flour
- 80 grams tapioca flour
- 80 grams potato starch
- 14 grams salt

Calories	330
Carbohydrates	60g
Protein	5g
Fat	9g
Fiber	7g

Prepare the preferment

1. In a bowl, mix 50g of active gluten-free sourdough starter, 100g sorghum flour, and 100g warm water. Gradually add the water to achieve a thick paste-like consistency.
2. Cover the bowl loosely and let the preferment sit at room temperature for 6-10 hours, or until it reaches its peak.

Prepare the dough

3. When the preferment is ready, prepare the psyllium gel. In a medium bowl, vigorously whisk the psyllium husk with water for 30-60 seconds until fully incorporated. Let the mixture sit for about 5-10 minutes to fully hydrate and develop a gel-like texture.
4. In a large bowl or stand mixer, whisk together the flours, starches and salt. Ensure these ingredients are thoroughly mixed for even distribution.
5. Add the preferment to the psyllium gel. Mix thoroughly by hand, with a wooden spoon, or using an electric mixer until the mixture is smooth and well combined.
6. Add the psyllium-preferment gel mixture to the dry ingredients and then add the oil. If using a stand mixer with a dough hook or mixing by hand with a large spoon or spatula, start combining the ingredients until a dough begins to form. Knead the dough until it is smooth and all ingredients are fully incorporated.
7. Turn the dough out onto a lightly floured surface and using a bench scraper or knife, divide it into 5 equal pieces, each weighing about 240g. Lightly oil your hands to prevent sticking, then shape each piece into a ball. Place the dough balls on an oil greased oven tray and cover them with a tea towel, let them proof for 3-5 hours.

Bake

8. About 1 hour before baking, place a baking steel, a pizza stone, or a pizza pan on the middle oven rack and preheat the oven to 500°F (250°C).
9. Generously grease a sheet of parchment paper and place a risen dough ball on top. Gently use your fingers to press and stretch the dough from the center outwards, until it reaches a thickness of about 1/8 inch (3-4mm).
10. Brush a light layer of olive oil on the surface of the pizza. Grab the sides of the parchment paper with the pizza on top and carefully transfer it, parchment paper and all, onto the preheated baking steel, pizza stone, or pizza pan. Bake for about 10-15 minutes, or until the crust is golden brown.
11. Remove from the oven, add your favorite toppings, and return to the oven for another 5-10 minutes. Take it out and serve hot.

PRETZELS

Yield: 6 pretzels

For the preferment
- 30 grams active gluten-free sourdough starter
- 60 grams millet flour
- 60 grams warm water (75-83°F / 24-28°C)

For the dough
- 22 grams whole psyllium husk
- 300 grams water
- 20 grams honey
- 120 grams sorghum flour
- 40 grams brown rice flour
- 70 grams tapioca flour
- 70 grams potato starch
- 6 grams salt

For the baking soda bath
- 8 cups of water
- 70 grams baking soda

To finish
- 1 egg yolk whisked with 1 tsp of water (egg wash)
- Flaky sea salt

Calories	230
Carbohydrates	44g
Protein	4g
Fat	3g
Fiber	5g

Prepare the preferment

1. In a bowl, mix 30g of active gluten-free sourdough starter, 60g millet flour, and 60g warm water. Gradually add the water to achieve a thick paste-like consistency.
2. Cover the bowl loosely and let the preferment sit at room temperature for 6-10 hours, or until it reaches its peak.

Prepare the dough

3. When the preferment is ready, prepare the psyllium gel. In a medium bowl, vigorously whisk the psyllium husk with water for 30-60 seconds until fully incorporated. Let the mixture sit for about 5-10 minutes to fully hydrate and develop a gel-like texture.
4. In a large bowl or stand mixer, whisk together the flours, starches and salt. Ensure these ingredients are thoroughly mixed for even distribution.
5. Add the preferment and the honey to the psyllium gel. Mix thoroughly by hand, with a wooden spoon, or using an electric mixer until the mixture is smooth and well combined.
6. Add the psyllium-preferment gel mixture to the dry ingredients. If using a stand mixer with a dough hook or mixing by hand with a large spoon or spatula, start combining the ingredients until a dough begins to form. Knead the dough until it is smooth and all ingredients are fully incorporated.

7. Line an oven tray with parchment paper and lightly spray it with nonstick cooking spray. Set aside. Divide the dough into 6 equal pieces, each weighing about 130g. Lightly oil your hands to prevent sticking, then roll each piece of dough into an 18-20 inch (45-50cm) rope and shape it into a "U." Cross the two ends over each other twice to form a twist. Fold the twisted part down onto the rounded "U" shape and gently press the ends down to form a pretzel shape.
8. Carefully transfer each pretzel to the prepared baking sheet. Repeat with the remaining dough, cover with a tea towel and let them proof for 1-3 hours.

Bake

9. After the pretzels have risen, place them in the freezer on the baking sheet for 10-15 minutes.
10. While the pretzels chill, preheat your oven to 445°F (230°C).
11. Bring 8 cups of water to a boil in a large pot, ensuring there's enough room since the baking soda will cause the water to foam up once added.
12. As the water heats, line a baking sheet with parchment paper and spray it with non-stick spray.
13. Once the water reaches a boil, carefully stir in the baking soda.
14. Remove the pretzels from the freezer, and using a slotted spoon, gently lower one pretzel into the boiling water. Let it cook for 25-30 seconds, turning it halfway through. Avoid boiling for more than 30 seconds, as it may give the pretzels a metallic flavor. Once done, take the pretzel out and place it on the prepared baking sheet. Repeat for all the pretzels.
15. After all the pretzels have been boiled, brush them with the egg wash and sprinkle some flaky sea salt. Use a sharp knife or blade to score the thickest part of the pretzels.
16. Place the baking sheet in the preheated oven and bake for 15-20 minutes, or until the pretzels are nicely golden brown. The internal temperature should reach 210°F (100°C), and a toothpick inserted should come out with minimal raw dough sticking to it. Once baked, let the pretzels cool on the baking sheet for 5 minutes before transferring them to a cooling rack to cool completely for at least 2 hours.

CONCLUSION & BONUS

Thank you for joining me on this journey into the world of gluten-free sourdough. I hope that through these pages, you have found both the knowledge and the confidence to craft delicious loaves that bring joy to your kitchen and beyond.

This book is more than a guide; it is an invitation to explore, experiment, and discover what works best for you. Sourdough is about patience, care, and celebrating small wins— values that are just as rewarding as the bread itself.

As you continue baking, remember that each loaf tells a story of your growth. Embrace the challenges and savor every success. I wish you many flavorful bakes, happy moments shared, and a lasting love for the magic of sourdough.

If you found this book helpful, I would be incredibly grateful if you could take a moment to leave a review on Amazon. Your feedback not only helps me improve but also assists others in discovering the joy of gluten-free sourdough baking. Thank you for your support!

Diane Romano

BONUS

GLUTEN-FREE SOURDOUGH DISCARD

Reduce Waste, Bake More:
50+ Sour-Flavored Recipes for Every Meal, Boosting Flavor and Nutrition

Made in the USA
Monee, IL
23 December 2024

75241969R00044